PUBLIC HOUSING:
CURRENT TRENDS AND FUTURE DEVELOPMENTS

Public Housing : Current Trends And Future Developments

EDITED BY
DAVID CLAPHAM
AND
JOHN ENGLISH

CROOM HELM
London • Sydney • Wolfeboro, New Hampshire

© 1987 David Clapham and John English
Croom Helm Ltd, Provident House, Burrell Row,
Beckenham, Kent, BR3 1AT

Croom Helm Australia, 44-50 Waterloo Road,
North Ryde, 2113, New South Wales

Public housing: current trends and future
  developments.
  1. Public housing — Great Britain
  I. Clapham, David II. English, John, *1944-*
  363.5'8   HD7288.78.G7

ISBN 0-7099-4826-3

Croom Helm, 27 South Main Street,
Wolfeboro, New Hampshire 03894-2069, USA

Library of Congress Cataloging-in-Publication Data

Public housing.

  1. Public housing — Great Britain. 2. Rental housing —
Great Britain. I. Clapham, David. II. English, John,
1944-
HDk7288.78.G7P783 1987   363.5'8   86-24056
ISBN 0-7099-4826-3

**Printed and bound in Great Britain
by Billing & Sons Limited, Worcester.**

CONTENTS

CONTRIBUTORS

David Clapham: Assistant   Director,   Centre   for
                             Housing   Research,   University   of
                             Glasgow.

John English: Lecturer   in Social Policy, Paisley
                             College.

Michael Foulis: Scottish Office.

Ray Forrest: Research Fellow, School for Advanced
                             Urban Studies, and Lecturer, School
                             of Applied Social Studies, University
                             of Bristol.

Chris Hamnett: Lecturer   in   Geography,   Open
                             University.

Michael Harloe: Senior   Lecturer,   Department   of
                             Sociology, University of Essex.

David McCulloch: Institute of Housing.

Alan Murie: Senior Lecturer, School for Advanced
                             Urban Studies, University of Bristol.

Bill Randolph: Assistant Research Officer, National
                             Federation of Housing Associations.

The origins of this book lie in a number of articles examining the current and future role of public rented housing in Britain which were published in the Housing Review in 1982 and 1983. The first of them (English, 1982) discussed changes in the public rented sector and used the term 'residualisation' to describe them. That article sparked off three others which looked at the nature and significance of these changes (Clapham and MacLennan, 1983; Malpass, 1983; Robinson and O'Sullivan, 1983). It was subsequently decided to hold a conference at the University of Glasgow in 1984 in order to build on this exchange of views in discussion with policymakers and administrators as well as with academic housing specialists. The conference was mainly concerned with the concept of residualisation, its meaning and how it could be measured. The mechanisms by which these changes had been brought about were also examined: most importantly the sale of council housing under the right-to-buy provisions of the Housing Act, 1980 (and the Tenants' Rights, Etc. (Scotland) Act, 1980), and the financial measures which had restricted new building and decreased revenue subsidies in the public sector. In addition, attention was focused on the relationship of residualisation to changes in the economic, political and social structure of Britain.

Although there was considerable interest in the issues raised at the conference, which were thought to be both important and timely, it was felt by some participants that, by focusing primarily on past trends, it did not deal adequately with the question of the future shape and form of the public sector. This was seen as especially interesting because of the number of experiments which were being initiated with new forms of public rented housing, such as those at Stockbridge Village near Liverpool and proposals for co-operatives in Glasgow. It was therefore decided to commission the chapters for this book with two objectives in mind. The first was to build on the conference discussions in order to review recent trends in public sector housing in

Preface

Britain and to discuss problems of measurement and interpretation. Within this objective the most important aim was to place the trends in context, both in terms of similar processes in other advanced Western countries and of the economic, social and political structure of Britain. The second objective was to examine the effects of these trends on the style of management of public rented housing with a particular focus on radical changes such as the creation of co-operatives and trusts.

Policy changes and socio-economic trends affecting the housing system during the last few years are charted, and the book brings together research findings which should be of interest in pointing to possible future developments in public sector housing. Although there are clues which can be drawn from recent experience in attempting to chart the likely course of such developments, any conclusions are inevitably speculative. It is hoped, however, that the book will provide a contribution to the debate about the role of public sector housing, and provoke further much needed discussion amongst policy-makers, administrators and academics.

The editors would like to acknowledge the help of Madhu Satsangi who compiled the index and of Georgina Barr who prepared the manuscript for publication.

Chapter One

THE CHANGING PUBLIC SECTOR

John English

The evolving role of the main tenures - the public sector, owner occupation and private renting - has long been recognised as a key factor in the operation of a nation's housing system; and what is happening to the tenure structure in Britain in the mid-1980s, with a particular focus on the changing role of the public sector, is the concern of this book. But an examination of the public sector - or of council housing, for in Britain the two terms are almost synonymous - necessarily also requires that a good deal of attention is given to complementary changes affecting the other main tenure of owner occupation. Less will be said about the private rented sector, if only because of its very small size in most of the country. Tenure is important, perhaps more so in Britain than in many other countries, because whether a house is owner-occupied or rented from a public authority or private landlord is fundamental in determining the rights and obligations of residents. Above all this is true of the entirely different bases on which financial assistance from the exchequer is available to meet a proportion of housing costs. Tenure is also related to other issues such as the quality of accommodation enjoyed (owner occupation tends to provide the best and private renting the worst standards), basis of access (whether by ability to pay or according to housing need) and constraints on mobility.

CHANGING TENURE PATTERNS

The size and function of different housing tenures, in the sense of which social groups they accommodate, has never been stable. The private rented sector has been declining continuously from its position of overwhelming dominance at the end of the first world war until, although it is still of some importance in certain areas and sub-markets, in overall terms it has become relatively insignificant with only nine per cent of the total stock in 1984. For some 60 years up to the late 1970s there were two major dynamic tenures in Britain, owner occupation and the public sector. The share of each sector in new building fluctuated so that their rate of growth varied, but both grew continuously. Since 1979, however, the public sector has been in absolute decline, as sales into owner occupation under the impetus of the Conservative government's right-to-buy legislation have exceeded a diminished rate of new building. The public sector reached its maximum share of the stock in the late 1970s with about 32 per cent over Britain as a whole; by 1984 it was already down to 28 per cent. In the same year owner occupation reached nearly 61 per cent of the stock (Department of the Environment, 1985) and seemed set to rise a good deal further. In 1985 the Secretary of State for the Environment spoke of 70 per cent of houses in Britain being owner occupied within ten years (Jenkin, 1985), a not unrealistic expectation given the high level of demand for the tenure, especially among new households. Survey evidence indicated that in the early 1980s over 80 per cent of younger people regarded owner occupation as their ideal housing tenure in two years' time (Building Societies Association, 1983). Interestingly, an even higher proportion expected to be owner occupiers in ten years' time, which perhaps suggests that some people feel constrained to enter the tenure because of the lack of acceptable alternatives. The growth of owner occupation has been based to a significant extent on the sale of private rented housing, but this source has diminished, from around 70,000 units a year in the 1960s and 1970s (Department of the Environment, 1977) to some 50,000 in the early 1980s (Inquiry into British Housing, 1985). By the latter period owner occupation was benefitting more than ever before from transfers of formerly rented housing but this was now predominantly, by a ratio of two or three to one, ex-council housing. In the early 1980s council house sales were almost as large a source of additional owner-occupied units as new building and were substantially more important in 1982 (Department of the Environment 1985; Scottish Development Department, 1985). Indeed, council house sales are essential if owner occupation is to continue to enjoy anything like the rate of growth it has experienced for much of the twentieth century, given the modest level of new construction in recent years and the likelihood that transfers from the private rented sector will be further reduced.

Not only is the relative size of the two tenures changing; so are the characteristics of people living in each and of the accommodation available to them. In its early years as a significant tenure, in the 1920s, the public sector catered mainly for the elite of the working class; then in the 1930s a rapid growth in owner occupation was accompanied by a switch in council building to rehousing poorer households under slum clearance schemes, often in markedly lower quality accommodation than that provided in the previous decade. Although general needs building predominated again after 1945, the removal of the restriction of council housing to the 'working classes' in 1949 was essentially symbolic; indeed, the tenure has always been dominated by manual workers and their families. But into the 1960s council housing was the goal of the majority of working class families in much of the country. Commentators on housing policy (for example Donnison, 1967) pointed out that the public sector was dominated by 'average' working class families, while the unskilled, the elderly and other disadvantaged groups were concentrated in low quality private rented housing. This is no longer the case, certainly not at the cutting edge of new households entering the housing market for the first time, and increasingly less so with the public sector as a whole. More and more the households of skilled and semi-skilled manual workers are joining the middle classes as owner occupiers, a trend which has been accelerated by the council house sales. At the same time, it is the relatively deprived who are replacing the more affluent in the public sector; they are now getting access to council housing, albeit often of indifferent quality (Murie, 1983). Indeed, had this not happened, given the decline of the private rented sector, the position of poorer households would be extremely bleak.

RESIDUALISATION OF THE PUBLIC SECTOR

These trends have been referred to as the 'residualisation' of public sector housing or, from a slightly different perspective focusing on the inter-relationship of tenures rather than on changes within the public sector, as the social 'polarisation' of housing tenures. Attention has been drawn to the increasing coincidence between council housing and what may loosely be called the relatively poor or deprived, and between owner occupation and the non-poor. The argument is basically that, with the effects of a low level of new building, inadequate maintenance and the sale of substantial numbers of predominantly better quality houses, the public sector more and more provides poor accommodation for poor households which are unable to achieve the 'normal' tenure of owner occupation. The weight of evidence, in this book and elsewhere, leaves no real doubt about the broad pattern of developments even if there are differences of view about details. But tenure polarisation has wider ramifications, because owner occupation, except perhaps right at the bottom of the market, brings with it many social and economic advantages, such as diminishing real housing costs, credit-worthiness and the accumulation of wealth. None of these advantages is shared by council tenants who are poor to start with and have fewer opportunities for improving their

position.   One function of the sale of council houses is to
give some of the more affluent of the present generation of
tenants, who with hindsight may feel that they made the
'wrong' choice of tenure in the past, a means by which they
are enabled to quit a less eligible status and join the more
eligible one of home owners.

Although the residualisation of council housing and
the polarisation of tenures have undoubtedly speeded up since
the Conservatives came to power in 1979, reflecting a greatly
increased rate of sales under the right-to-buy provisions of
the Housing Act, 1980 and drastic reductions in investment in
public sector building, the processes have their origins in
the 1960s if not before.   Owner occupiers have long enjoyed
great financial advantages in the long term even if initially
they face relatively high costs.   The almost complete
removal of exchequer assistance to council tenants since 1979
(except for means-tested housing benefit available only to
those on low incomes) has only served to increase the
existing financial advantages of ownership for the majority
of households.   It would, indeed, be amazing were the role
of the public sector not changing.

What has been and is happening may be thought to
have both positive and negative aspects.   On the positive
side the fact that more deprived sections of society now have
effective access to what is on the whole reasonable housing
in the public sector - and certainly almost always an
improvement on what the private rented sector used to provide
- must be counted as progress.   The public sector has also
been the main provider of purpose-built accommodation
designed to meet the special needs of the elderly and the
handicapped.   On the other hand, the creation of 'welfare'
housing in the public sector, from which the most attractive
accommodation is being lost as a result of sales, may in
itself not be counted as a gain.   Perhaps Aneurin Bevan's
vision in the 1940s, when the restriction of council housing
to the working classes was removed, of a public sector which
would cater for a wide social spectrum was never very
realistic; but the opposite extreme of often unattractive
and flatted estates containing only those who are too poor to
achieve owner occupation, if all too realistic, is not
particularly appealing.   With a drying up of reasonably
priced accommodation in the private rented sector, and
perhaps a continuing propensity to leave the parental home
earlier, younger people, for example students, will probably
make growing use of the public sector; but the fact that
they are transient rather than deprived is unlikely to make a
great deal of difference to the overall picture.

Issues in housing policy in both the political and
academic spheres, as in most fields, change over time.   In
the 1970s and early 1980s a great deal of attention was given
to council house sales; but the principle of sales, which
has been accepted even if reluctantly by the Labour Party, is

no longer much of a political issue (although analysis of their effects continues to be important). Then the residualisation of council housing came to the fore in academic debates; but another issue which emerged into prominence in 1985 and 1986, as much at the political as the academic level, relates to criticism of traditional local authority management of the public sector and to proposals for various forms of co-operatives, trusts and privatisation measures apart from individual purchase for owner occupation under the right to buy. The importance of initiatives of this kind from the government's point of view was signalled in 1985 by the formation within the Department of the Environment of the Urban Housing Renewal Unit and by the speech of the then Secretary of State, Patrick Jenkin, to the annual conference of the Institute of Housing (Jenkin, 1985). The Housing and Planning Bill, which is passing through parliament during 1986, includes provisions to facilitate the transfer of management functions from local authorities to independent bodies, and the compulsory rehousing of tenants where estates are sold for rehabilitation. Such initiatives, which have already begun on a modest scale, could radically alter much of the remaining public sector over a period of years. As well as the possibilities for the 'mass privatisation' of public rented housing, attention is also focused on the management of remaining council estates. Few would deny that housing management has had major shortcomings, but in the future it will have to deal with a public sector increasingly dominated by less successful and unpopular estates, often consisting of flats, and by tenants with a disproportionate share of economic and social problems.

ACCESS AND MOBILITY

In this introductory chapter, before outlining the topics covered in the book, it is worth mentioning two problematic aspects of public sector housing which are not dealt with elsewhere. These are, first, access to the public sector and allocation policies; and, second, opportunities for mobility across local authority boundaries. What may be seen as shortcomings in both areas, at least from the point of view of many relatively non-deprived households, arguably tend to reinforce the residualisation of public housing.

Access to the Public Sector

There has been a considerable body of research and discussion on allocation policies in recent years, in particular in relation to the question of who gets what in terms of housing quality (see, for example, English, forthcoming; Henderson and Karn, 1986). The tendency for households with little bargaining power, for example because

of urgent need, to be allocated less popular accommodation is
deeply rooted; but many housing authorities now attempt to
avoid this happening by giving greater weight to housing
need. Desirable as need may be as a criterion for priority,
it does nothing to enable public housing also to respond to
demands and aspirations, and may indeed make doing so more
difficult with implications for the continued residualisation
of the sector. Even if standards of service in council
housing were to be radically improved, and leaving aside the
long-term financial penalties suffered by tenants compared
with owner occupiers, because of dilemmas in the field of
allocation it is doubtful how far council housing could be
successful in attracting and satisfying the aspirations of
households which are not obliged to rent. Financial
arrangements cannot, of course, be ignored and, if a more
even-handed approach to owning and renting is unlikely to be
forthcoming, significant numbers of those with choice are
unlikely to consider the public sector in any case.
Nevertheless, some might be interested in renting for limited
periods when purchase is not really convenient, for example
for the duration of a temporary job. The problems inherent
in allocating and pricing social rented housing if it were to
cater for demands as well as need raise complex issues (see,
for example, English, 1982a; Webster, 1981). In brief, the
public sector has traditionally been oriented towards meeting
officially-defined 'needs', and finds it hard to come to
terms with the aspirations of those who can exercise
choice. Access to better-quality housing in preferred
locations is usually on the basis of a lengthy wait or,
sometimes, a high level of needs-based priority. There can
be little doubt that the failure to provide ready access to
desirable housing for what are seen as low priority
households, because of a concern, admirable in itself, with
fairness and meeting basic needs, has been a factor in
residualisation of the public sector.

A quotation from one of the articles mentioned
above may serve to crystallise the point (English, 1982a,
p.155).

> Say that a household without any urgent housing
> need would like to rent a council house. The
> family applies to the local authority for a house
> which meets both their needs and aspirations.
> What then is likely to be their reaction if they
> are told: 'Your need is slight and the only
> accommodation which we can offer you is a
> difficult-to-let flat'? Surely they will then
> decide that, despite their preference for
> renting, only owner occupation can provide them
> with a house which meets their aspirations. They
> are likely to be attracted by political

programmes for the further extension of owner occupation, the sale of council housing, and the limitation of the public sector to a residual role. And will not their experience have confirmed the anti-council housing case: that it is ill-adapted to do more than meeting basic needs and should be confined to this function?

But an attempt to meet demands as well as needs would pose awkward questions about, for example, the desirability of a quasi-market pricing system which attempts to set rents so as to equilibrate supply and demand for popular housing, and the danger that this might increase the problem of deprived ghetto estates. Nevertheless, it is perhaps significant that proponents of public housing have not engaged in this debate to any great extent, either to criticise propositions of the kind outlined here or to explore how the sector could meet both needs and demands. It may be that public housing really is inherently unsuited to catering for the aspirations of a broad section of society and that it should confine itself essentially to those who have little choice. This is, of course, essentially the view underlying the policies of the present Conservative government.

Mobility within the Public Sector

Another weakness of the public sector, which is also linked with allocation policies, is mobility. While council housing has reasonably effective mechanisms for mobility within a local authority area through transfer arrangements, longer distance mobility is much more difficult. The position has been improved to some extent since the establishment of the National Mobility Scheme, in which virtually all local authorities now participate, while the barriers to movement within the owner-occupied sector created by transaction costs and wide regional variations in house prices should not be underestimated. But the council tenant generally still finds it a good deal less easy to move from area to area than does the owner occupier. The National Mobility Scheme requires households to have a 'legitimate' reason for wanting to move, related to employment or the provision of social support, while the recently established Tenants' Exchange Scheme is dependent upon the vagaries of finding someone with whom to do a swap. The problem of mobility in the public sector is, of course, another aspect of access to housing, and of the assumption that, except in the case of low standard and unpopular accommodation, people should either have a high level of officially recognised need or wait a long time before being accommodated.

A further consideration relating to mobility, which causes some commentators to advocate a reduction in the size of the public sector and the expansion of owner occupation, is the argument that difficulties moving across local authority boundaries deter people from considering jobs in other areas, and are therefore harmful to the economy and increase unemployment. There may be some truth in this view, although the problems caused by wide disparities in house prices have already been mentioned. There is also a need for research on the effectiveness of the National Mobility Scheme.

OUTLINE OF THE BOOK

Within the broad themes of the polarisation of housing tenure, the residualisation of the public sector and prospects for its future, the authors examine a variety of more specific topics. In chapter 2 Murie looks at the historical background: at how council housing has changed from catering mainly for the affluent employed working class to increasingly sheltering the poor and economically marginal. While the former have been moving into owner occupation, the latter have been largely taken over from the declining private rented sector. There has also been a parallel social polarisation of the population with the growth of low paid work and unemployment. The co-incidence of a disadvantaged tenure - council housing - with other aspects of deprivation, Murie suggests, exacerbates the latter. There is then an examination of the spatial dimension of polarisation - particularly differences between the inner and outer city - which aggregate statistics hide. Evidence from London and Liverpool shows a sharpening of the polarisation process through a concentration of council house sales in outer rather than inner areas, and on houses rather than flats.

Hamnett and Randolph take up related themes in chapter 3, in a detailed study of socio-tenurial polarisation and the social residualisation of council housing in inner London. They focus on how these processes can be measured, and their data, which are derived from 1981 census small area statistics, relate to areas of public sector housing in Lambeth and Camden. How far the processes reflect the operation of the housing system and how far changes in the labour market is uncertain, but they conclude that in terms of income, socio-economic group and unemployment the council sector accommodated a higher proportion of the economically marginal in 1981 compared with ten years previously.

Chapter 4 is concerned with perhaps the single most important causative factor, at least as far as government policy is concerned, in polarisation and residualisation, the treatment of the public and owner-occupied sectors in terms of subsidies and taxation. McCulloch concentrates on the policies of the Conservative government since 1979 towards exchequer assistance to, and capital spending by, the public sector. The favoured treatment of owner occupation has, of course, existed for many years, but Mrs. Thatcher's government has greatly widened the disparity between the two tenures by obliging local authorites sharply to increase the proportion of outgoings met by rents, thus forcing them up far ahead of the rate of inflation, until the majority of councils in England are now making surpluses on their housing. There has been an enormous increase in dependence on means-tested assistance through housing benefit, while there is growing pressure on non-poor households to purchase their council house or not to enter the tenure in the first place.

In chapter 5 Forrest places another policy of the Conservative government since 1979, of encouraging council house sales on the largest possible scale, in the context of the broader privatisation of state assets and a general restructuring of welfare provision towards a residual role. The pattern of sales in five local areas is then examined. Forrest makes the point that the redistribution of wealth to individual households, implicit in council house purchase at a substantial discount, varies enormously from area to area depending on the level of house prices. Furthermore, with steep rises in council rents, in addition to the effects of discounts, owning may no longer be more expensive, even initially, than renting. Thus in some localities council house purchase is often motivated primarily by a desire merely to escape rising costs.

Chapter 6, based on data collected by the Scottish Development Department, looks at council house sales in Scotland in the period following the introduction of the right to buy in 1980. Foulis examines both the spatial distribution of sales and the type of dwellings which are likely to be bought. He concludes that sales in the early 1980s tended to be spread through a range of areas but to be predominantly of better types of property, especially houses rather than flats. It also seems likely, despite the effects of sales and a depressed rate of new construction in the public sector, that Scotland will continue to have a markedly lower level of owner occupation than exists south of the border.

Chapter 7 moves on to the implications for housing administration of the residualisation of the public sector. Poorer tenants and higher rents are likely to exacerbate the arrears problem, while disrepair of the stock may get worse if severe restraints on public expenditure continue. Housing management staff will probably find themselves working more closely with other arms of the welfare state, such as social security and health services. Clapham argues that local authority housing management tends to be both inefficient and paternalistic, and that this has contributed to residualisation. He distinguishes three models of housing management which have emerged and discusses their possible role in the future: a contractual approach, emphasising efficiency and a businesslike relationship with tenants; housing management as welfare work, implying decentralisation and a higher level of personal contact with tenants; and tenant self-management which is being brought about, for example, through management co-operatives.

A comparative perspective is introduced in chapter 8, where Harloe examines social rented housing in Europe. Direct public provision of housing is rare in other European countries, where the use of non-profit organisations such as housing associations and co-operatives is usual. These enjoy greater independence from government than do local housing authorities in Britain and neither are distinctions between different categories of rented housing so clear cut. But similarities between Britain and the rest of Europe are sufficient for it to be possible to detect the same sort of trends in both, in particular government policies which focus on the promotion of owner occupation and a downgrading of the contribution of social rented housing.

Finally, chapter 9 looks at the options that are likely to be open to the public sector in Britain by focusing on some of the more important initiatives now being applied to it. The policy of individual sales under the right to buy is now well established, effectively accepted by all the main political parties, and has probably passed its peak in numerical terms. The initiatives which Clapham discusses are decentralisation of housing management by local authorities, mass privatisation where whole estates are sold, usually as empty houses, to developers for improvement and resale to owner occupiers; and various forms of trusts. These may be formed on the bases of common ownership by tenants in a more radical version of management co-operatives, though in some cases, such as the pioneer Stockbridge Village Trust in Knowsley near Liverpool, financial institutions providing capital for purchase and improvement appear to have a predominant role. Privatisation removes housing from the public sector, but whether it increases residualisation of the public sector will depend on its particular form. The disposal of unpopular and stigmatised estates to developers for improvement and resale to owner occupiers is unlikely to do so, though the sale of apparently good quality housing, as has happened with Langbaurgh's Spencerbeck estate in North East England (Cowan, 1985), must surely tend to have this effect. The other initiatives can perhaps be seen as ways in which the residualisation process might be slowed, by providing a better quality of service that is more able to compete with owner occupation. But in the absence of radical changes to financial support to, and taxation of, different tenures, of which there seems little prospect in the foreseeable future, Clapham concludes that reforms of housing administration in the public sector will not reverse or even halt the trends which are identified throughout the book.

The argument which is developed in the book, therefore, is that the polarisation of tenures and the residualisation of the public sector constitute one of the most significant changes now taking place in the British housing system, a trend which is also occurring in other European countries. The focus is chiefly on the effects of polarisation and residualisation, on council house sales as an important mechanism through which the process operates, and on the future of the remaining public sector. Causative factors are dealt with less comprehensively, although recent subsidy policies, a particularly important one, are reviewed in some detail. The all too frequent failure of housing management in the public sector to provide a high standard of efficient and responsive service to tenants is also touched on in looking at new approaches which may replace traditional local authority administration. In the past, developments in management within the public sector and in new forms of tenure have been largely based on local initiatives, but with the establishment of the Priority Estates Project in 1979, and more recently of the Urban Housing Renewal Unit, central government is taking an increasingly exhortatory if not directive role in these areas.

It is probably now too late for any feasible measures of policy or administration to make a great deal of difference in that polarisation and residualisation are so firmly established and advanced. In reality the main pressure for change on housing administration is likely to be to adapt to a more welfare-oriented role. An increasingly large proportion of public sector tenants will be elderly, handicapped, or otherwise incapable of an adequate level of social functioning without support. The present government, as well as enthusiastically promoting sales, emphasise that new local authority building should be confined to meeting special needs. The likelihood is, therefore, that the public sector will continue to diminish in size and to be transmuted very largely into a welfare service for the relatively poor. This trend seems not only inexorable but almost inevitable; whether it is desirable is a question on which opinions can legitimately differ.

Chapter Two

SOCIAL POLARISATION AND HOUSING PROVISION

Alan Murie

        Much of the current discussion of the future of the
public sector in housing has focused on the tendency for
council housing to become a residual or welfare housing
sector.   This tendency has been widely discussed elsewhere
(English, 1982a; Forrest and Murie, 1983;   Malpass, 1983;
Murie, 1983).   It is generally accepted that such a tendency
and the elements of change referred to in the context of
residualisation are not just a product of the Housing Act,
1980 but also of longer trends, and of investment and
financial decisions made a considerable time ago.   However,
the Housing Act, 1980 has focused attention on the changing
roles of different tenures and has arguably speeded up
certain changes.   The debate about residualisation does not
necessarily only refer to council housing.   It has, however,
tended to be linked with a picture of a developing
polarisation of the two major tenures.   It is this
polarisation which leaves the public sector with a more
distinctive role, catering for the marginal poor.   Reference
to tenure categories in this kind of debate has both
advantages and disadvantages.   It enables a clear focus in
terms for which data are available, and tenure divisions do
relate to very different systems of negotiating access to
housing.   However, a preoccupation with tenure should not
lead to a neglect of other elements in housing inequality.
Discussion of tenure polarisation highlights certain aspects
of change but should not be used to obscure others.   It
should be set against an historical, institutional and
financial background of state sponsorship for owner
occupation.   It should also relate to the broader analysis
of social polarisation, and it should be set in a context in
which the two principal tenures ought not to have the terms
'public' and 'private' sectors attached to them.   Owner
occupation has in many ways become the public sector.   While
it is council housing which is publicly owned, it is the
owner-occupied sector .which, in financial, political and
ideological terms, represents the ambitions of state
intervention in the housing market.

12

Social Polarisation and Housing Provision

The social composition of the major housing tenures in Britain is constantly changing. The organisation of housing has altered so markedly over the present century that this is hardly surprising, but the nature and direction of change raise a number of questions. Is council housing failing to provide for those in most need, or failing to achieve social mix? Are the financial and other benefits of owner occupation failing to reach certain sections of the population? Do policies which benefit different tenures effectively benefit sections of the community with particular advantages or disadvantages in other respects? Are the different housing qualities and standards provided in different tenures taken advantage of by a cross-section of the population, or are certain groups more likely to live in high rise flats or in detached dwellings because of their distribution between tenures?

There is also a series of wider questions. What has been the impact of the wider and deeper support for owner occupation in recent years, and of the erosion of public support and acceptability of council housing associated with high rise building and with the political, ideological and financial attacks on the sector? How far do the opportunities to accumulate and store wealth through housing involve a redistribution of wealth, and how thorough a redistribution is involved? In a period of rising unemployment, in which social polarisation is a feature of the uneven impact of recession, what is the relationship between social polarisation and housing?

This chapter offers some background to these issues. It argues that the evidence of social polarisation between tenures is important and that reference to tenure polarisation is a valuable starting point in analysing housing trends. But we must avoid constructing a conventional wisdom around tenure polarisation, and, through this, neglect or obscure other important aspects of change in housing.

HISTORICAL BACKGROUND

The historical background to discussion of the social make-up of different tenures has been the shifting emphasis of public policy. At certain stages in its development, council housing has catered for the affluent employed working class rather than those who have been peripheral to economic development. In these periods it has been private renting which has catered for the poorest and those with least bargaining power. In periods when council housing was provided for 'poorer' households - especially in periods of slum clearance activity - the standards of accommodation involved tended to be reduced. Explanations for such alterations include those which refer to changes in the balance of class forces or in the power of organised

13

labour. Nevertheless, over the history of council housing - through different periods of development, with the decline of private renting and the increasing dominance of state provision in the rented market - and with changes in the circumstances of households over their lives as tenants, the council sector has achieved considerable social mix.

In owner occupation, family cycle, income and cost factors have similarly combined to produce a 'social mix' among owners. There have been periods in the development of owner occupation when access has been easier for lower income first time buyers - whether buying newly built homes or purchasing from landlords as sitting tenants. In more recent years in some localities the growth of owner occupation has principally occurred directly through state activity. Thus in Birmingham in the period 1971-80 some 9,570 dwellings were provided by private enterprise for sale, 15,560 council dwellings became owner occupied, and improvement for sale and other council schemes also increased owner occupation. In Liverpool, council house sales were the main contributor to the growth of owner occupation between 1970 and 1980 while building for sale by the local authority was considerable. Policies of this type have often been specifically targeted at 'poorer' households and those in need, and some have been partially successful in assisting these groups into owner occupation (see Forrest, Lansley and Murie, 1984). Property values in some, notably inner city, areas and in some regions have left house purchase within the reach of a variety of households. In other areas shortages of rented accommodation have 'forced' households to buy, in some cases leaving owners in a precarious, marginal situation. The evidence currently being discussed which suggests changes in this pattern of 'social mix' in the two main tenures and widening differences between who is in each tenure.

The debate around tenure polarisation has tended to develop from empirical observations about the changing composition of the two dominant tenures in the British housing market. It has tended, then, to involve a discussion of housing factors - the decline of private renting, mobility between tenures, access, changes in the quality of stock, relative costs and subsidies. What is missing (or perhaps taken for granted) in discussion is a wider background of social polarisation. There is a literature concerned with the impact of economic recession and high unemployment, changes and reductions in welfare provision and the weakening of organised labour. Progressive deskilling and unemployment have particularly affected those in unskilled manual work and the personal service sector. Permanent non-employment rather than temporary unemployment has become the experience of certain groups in some localities. The incomes of the temporarily or permanently unemployed are falling behind those in employment as a result of benefit cuts. Those in low paid employment have experienced lower rates of wage increase than the average. The marginal or peripheral sections of the labour force are expanding as a consequence of economic recession, technological restructuring and demographic change.

The official unemployment figure in the mid-1980s was over three million and this excluded recent school leavers, those in training schemes and a high proportion of unemployed women. It represented around 13 per cent of the workforce as officially defined. These figures are, however, subject to considerable variation. Manufacturing industry has suffered the most marked decline, accounting for 35 per cent of jobs in Britain in 1951 but only 27 per cent in 1981 (Anderson et al, 1983). It is those areas dominated by traditional manufacturing industry such as steel and shipbuilding which have suffered most, and this decline has been concentrated in the older industrial towns and the inner areas of the major cities. Massey (1983) observed that 200,000 manufacturing jobs were lost in the Greater London area every five years from 1961 to 1976. The decline of the British manufacturing sector which has been evident throughout this century has dramatically accelerated in the last few years. The West Midlands industrial core continued to experience an increase in manufacturing employment until the late 1970s but the decline of the British car industry, which was concentrated in that region, has since resulted in rapid job loss there. Between 1978 and 1982 the manufacturing workforce declined by 20 per cent. At the 1981 Census, male unemployment in some of Birmingham's inner city areas stood at 30 per cent. In Liverpool unemployment rates were nearing 40 per cent of economically active males (Office of Population Censuses and Surveys, 1982). By the end of 1983 average figures for male unemployment in the regions range from around twelve per cent in the South East and South West of England to 20 per cent in the West Midlands and the North of England. Northern Ireland recorded the highest rate of male unemployment in the UK at 27 per cent. There is strong North-South dimension to the impact of the recession. The centre of gravity of economic and social power has moved perceptibly towards the south, to Britain's 'sun belt' of relative affluence, and there is lower than average unemployment running along a motorway corridor from London to Bristol.

These observed spatial differences in the impact of economic decline combine with class and gender differentiation. Those in semi-skilled and unskilled work have suffered the most. It is against this background that tenure polarisation is significant. The fact that different tenures cater for households with different characteristics - and perhaps do so to an increasing extent - is of importance because of the different rights and opportunities carried with tenure status (including differences in dwelling type and in spatial location). The coincidence of tenure difference with other aspects of disadvantage, and the extent to which this coincidence exacerbates such wider disadvantages, are crucial.

A number of assertions could be made arising from this. First, it might be argued that tenure polarisation is not an issue in itself. An increasing concentration of particular groups in, say, council housing could be an 'equalising' phenomenon if the quality of housing service being provided was high (in relative and absolute terms) and if council housing increased access to other resources. Equally, a static or declining concentration of particular groups could involve a deepening of inequalities if the experience of that group in council housing was of increasing disadvantage and exclusion from the opportunities available to others. In this way it is important that discussion of tenure polarisation should not become a rarified exercise in manipulation of standardised data and measurements for its own sake. The interest in who is in different tenures and in patterns of change over time arises because of the differential impact of other social and economic changes and the experience of tenure. In this latter respect it is important to acknowledge that tenure is not a static category but rather has different and changing meanings and connotations.

In relation to council housing the current experience for many tenants is of declining quality, rising real costs and increasing disparity in quality and cost compared with home owners. The two major tenures differ markedly in what they provide in terms both of dwelling type and opportunities for capital accumulation. The increasing differentiation within both council housing and owner occupation is an important element in this comparison. In the discussion both of differences within and between tenures the spatial dimension is also of importance and this is returned to later in the chapter.

TENURE POLARISATION

Much discussion of social polarisation is conducted in broad aggregate categories of 'working class' or 'white collar' but such categories are not satisfactory if we are concerned to identify associations between the experience of tenure and experience in relation to incomes, employment or other aspects of social inequality. The socio-economic group (SEG) categories normally referred to in this debate are more appropriate because the experience of, say, semi-skilled or unskilled workers differs from that of skilled workers. More precise occupational categories would enable stronger connections to be made between the experience of occupational and economic change on the one hand and tenure change on the other - they would provide more robust indications of the degree of concentration in particular tenures of groups experiencing common problems in other respects. The experience of occupational categories grouped together in SEGs is divergent and the process of amalgamation obscures some patterns. Within the normal SEG categories there are sub groups with very different tenure characteristics. For example, junior non-manual workers are considerably less likely to be owner occupiers than the 'ancillary workers and artists' with whom they are lumped together (in the 1981 Census 66 per cent and 77 per cent owner occupiers respectively). Even with such detailed information it would be appropriate to add issues of income, numbers of earners and dependency on state benefits in a discussion of tenure polarisation.

A substantial amount of evidence provides a basis for discussion of tenure polarisation. This can broadly be summarised as follows:

Contrasting Social Profiles: Evidence from various sources restates differences in the social profiles of different tenures. While the different tenures have different profiles in terms of social class, income and household composition, there is also an interaction between these. For example, the likelihood of households being in council housing increases in successive SEG categories (from professional and managerial to unskilled); but within each SEG category households below the poverty line (conventionally defined as basic supplementary benefit scales plus 40 per cent) are more likely to be in council housing than those above it (Murie, 1983). Those groups which are most at risk in relation to the impact of economic recession are over-represented in council housing.

Data on Trends: Although there is evidence providing social profiles at particular times, data on SEG, incomes or those out of work and in receipt of supplementary benefit covering a longer time period may be preferred. The data on supplementary benefits refer to the period since 1967 (Table 2.1). It shows that as private renting has declined, households in receipt of supplementary benefit have become increasingly concentrated in the public sector. The falling proportion of supplementary benefit recipients in the private rented sector was, until 1975, wholly taken up by the public sector. Only since 1976 has there been any increase in the proportion of supplementary benefit recipients who are owner occupiers. And only in 1980 did the proportion of supplementary benefit recipients with mortgage interest included in their assessment rise (from 3.4 per cent of all cases in 1979 to 5.3 per cent in 1981). Relative to its role in the whole stock, owner occupation caters to a very limited extent for supplementary benefit recipients. Both the main rented sectors provide disproportionately for the poor, but it is incorrect to regard the private rented sector as the tenure used by the least affluent. If the public sector catered for supplementary benefit recipients on a pro rata basis with the private rented sector it would have housed 42 per cent of supplementary benefit recipients in 1971 and 53 per cent in 1976. The actual figures were 53 per cent in 1971 and 58 per cent in 1976. In these terms, it is the public sector which provides most intensively for those with low incomes, and while it may be argued that more of the poor should be catered for, some hesitation is needed in arguing that the public sector has failed in this respect. Nor is this pattern a result of the public sector catering disproportionately for particular groups of supplementary benefit recipients. Among recipients the majority of the elderly, the unemployed, the sick and disabled, and single parent families are all in local authority housing.

Family Expenditure Survey (FES) data indicate a rise in the proportion of households in the bottom three income deciles which were council tenants - from 26.3 per cent in 1963 to 47.0 per cent in 1979. More detailed analysis of FES data shows that between 1968 and 1978 this increase was particularly marked in the bottom decile where the proportion rose from 33 to 56 per cent. The proportion of households in each of the top five deciles which are in local authority housing has fallen in the same period. Single parent and retired household heads are particularly significant among those in the lower income deciles who are increasingly in council housing (Robinson and O'Sullivan, 1983).

Other analyses of data over time using FES and census data confirm this view of increasing social polarisation between the two main tenures. However, the most reliable comparisons in terms of SEG refer to relatively short time periods. Thus, for example, General Household Survey (GHS) data only refer to the period since 1972. But the GHS shows that in 1978 compared with 1972 a larger proportion of professionals, and skilled and unskilled workers, were owner occupiers; that a declining proportion of professionals, employers and managers and skilled workers were council or new town tenants; and that a larger proportion of semi-skilled and unskilled workers were council or new town tenants. Among the unskilled, the increased representation in council tenancy was six per cent compared with an increase of three per cent in owner occupation. These changes are sustained in 1979 GHS data.

Table 2.1:   Tenure of Supplementary Benefit Recipients
             1967–82

	Number (thousands)	Proportion of Recipients in Each Tenure		
		Owner Occupiers %	LA Tenants %	Tenants of Private Landlords %
1967	2154	17	45	38
1968	2223	17	47	36
1969	2296	17	49	34
1970	2329	17	51	32
1971	2471	17	53	30
1972	2475	17	55	28
1973	2292	17	56	27
1974	2268	17	58	25
1975	2261	17	57	25
1976	2328	18	58	24
1977	2432	19	59	22
1978	2420	18	60	21
1979	2342	19	61	20
1980	2462	19	61	19
1981	2869	19	61	19
1982	3208	19	62	18

Note: There have been changes in methods of estimation and
         slight variations in figures given for particular
         years.
Source: Department of Health and Social Security, Social
         Security Statistics, HMSO, annual.

Hamnett's (1984, p.397–8) discussion of census data
for England and Wales between 1961 and 1981 backs up this
picture and leads him to the conclusion that:

the semi-skilled and the unskilled have become
increasingly concentrated in the council sector
relative to the other SEGs. Although the
increase in owner-occupation over the period
percolated down to all SEGs, it became
increasingly diluted as it reached the lower
SEGs. By contrast, it was in these groups,
which also experienced the great decline in the
percentage of privately rented households, which
displayed the greatest increase in the proportion
of council tenants. Whilst we cannot
necessarily conclude that the privately rented

sector has differentially split as it has declined, in that households leaving private renting and those entering the other two tenures are not necessarily the same households, what is clear is that the decline in the privately rented sector has resulted in an intensifying degree of polarisation between the other two tenures over the last 20 years as a whole and over the last ten years in particular.

Household Movement: All of the evidence published in recent years on the movement of households indicates that moves between owner occupation and council housing are relatively rare; that the bulk of moves are within these tenures; and that both immobility and the direction of movement between tenures are linked to class, income and family cycle factors in a way which reinforces rather than diminishes the initial social split between tenures. Perhaps the most picturesque presentation of this evidence refers to the National Movers Survey 1972 and shows that movement between tenures makes the extent of segregation more marked; differences in the probability of different SEGs using the owner-occupied and public sectors become sharper (Murie, Niner and Watson, 1976). Figure 2.1 demonstrates that the proportion of households which are council tenants increases with successive SEG categories. This applies irrespective of poverty status although those below the poverty line used here are more likely to be council tenants and SEG variation is less for households in poverty.

The evidence from specific studies of newly formed households demonstrates a tendency for initial housing tenure to be related to economic and income circumstances as well as household composition. Analyses referring to poverty and to marriage and divorce reinforce the picture. Dunnell (1979) has reported that the most consistent factor affecting divorce patterns is age at time of marriage and this does vary by social class. There are more teenage marriages among manual workers, and young marriages have a higher propensity to end in divorce. Households in this situation are also more likely to be living in the parental home or to have recently entered some form of rented tenure. Middle class households experiencing marital breakdown are more likely to have married later, bought a house at time of marriage, acquired more household goods and delayed child bearing. In this study 39 per cent of professional households had bought a home at the time of marriage compared with less than ten per cent of households with unskilled heads. Indeed, more than half of the households in the latter category were still sharing accommodation at marriage. Contrasting pictures of the impact of marital break-up on households in different class locations but with similar marriage durations emerge from this. A number of

Figure 2.1: Proportion of Public Sector Tenants in SEG Categories According to Poverty Status

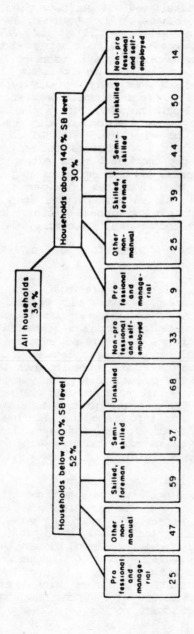

Poverty is defined as the appropriate supplementary scale rate plus 40 per cent.

Source: Murie (1983) (from General Household Survey, 1975)

other recent studies have elaborated on associations between income, fertility and social class in the early stages of housing careers. These factors strongly influence initial tenure and the likelihood of shifting from that tenure subsequently (see Holmans, 1981; Ineichen, 1980; Madge and Brown, 1981; Payne and Payne, 1977; Sullivan and Murphy, 1984). The evidence we have to construct housing careers suggests an increasing divergence in terms of tenure between groups who in the past had the same experience of tenure.

These various sources of evidence provide a strong base to assert that there is a split between the tenure of the employed, well-paid household often with more than one earner, and those out of employment with low earnings or incomes below the poverty line. In SEG tabulations this split is apparent at the extremes between, for example, professionals and the unskilled. The extent of this split has become more marked over recent years as private renting has declined and the advantages of owner occupation have increased. While skilled workers have increasingly moved into owner occupation, the semi-skilled, unskilled and 'marginal' poor are increasingly in council housing.

RESERVATIONS: SPATIAL DIMENSIONS AND DIFFERENCES WITHIN TENURES

The data referred to previously provide an average and aggregate picture. However, much of the discussion of trends in relation to housing and social polarisation is couched in terms of regional and inner/outer city problems. The most striking images of tenure polarisation are those of deprived inner city or peripheral estates and of affluent owner occupied suburbia. The aggregate data lack a spatial dimension. They are compatible with very different trends in different areas - with more dramatic changes in some and less in others. The aggregate picture is also deficient in another respect. Differences within housing tenures are considerable. A focus on tenure polarisation conjures an impression of two homogeneous tenures growing apart. It is in danger of understating differentiation and residualisation within tenures.

Observations for particular localities where council housing does not have the same connotations, or where owner occupation rather than council housing includes the worst housing generating least advantage, are not incompatible with the kind of analysis of tenure polarisation referred to above. However, they do suggest that when it is deprived of a spatial dimension discussion of tenure polarisation has a limited capacity to highlight differences and trends. Examination of tenure differences in specific localities is necessary to demonstrate variations in experience of the impact of economic change and changing housing circumstances, and the relationship to differentiation within tenures. It also provides the opportunity to consider the likely impact of current policies (including the sale of council houses) which could have the effect of reducing the extent to which tenure coincides with the various social attributes referred to earlier. Research material which would satisfy those interested in this issue is not generally available although there is some evidence which is not easily discounted; that evidence from recent research relating to Birmingham, Liverpool and London also develops different dimensions of this discussion (Forrest and Murie, forthcoming).

London

Since 1961 the geography of housing tenure in Greater London has been transformed. The decline of private renting, and growth of both council housing and owner occupation, have not taken place at an even pace throughout the area; an outer, predominantly owner-occupied, ring and an inner, predominantly rented, ring have emerged (see Hamnett, 1983a). In 1961 private renting was the dominant tenure in Greater London, accommodating almost half of all households. By 1981 more than half of London's private tenants had disappeared. This decline has occurred in both inner and outer London but from a different base - a decline from 64 per cent to 30 per cent in inner London and from 30 per cent to 15 per cent in outer London. But the growth of other tenures to replace private renting has been uneven. Owner occupation has expanded from 17 per cent to 27 per cent in inner London and in outer London from 53 per cent to 62 per cent. It is the public housing sector which has expanded much more rapidly in inner London; in 1981 it catered for 43 per cent of households compared with 23 per cent of those in outer London. Rather than the decline of private renting resulting in a levelling of home ownership rates between inner and outer London, the differential growth of council housing has left tenure differences as marked as 20 years before, but with council housing as the largest tenure in inner London. The distinctions are even sharper at borough level. In outer London only four boroughs had over 25 per cent of their households living in council housing. In inner London only one borough had fewer than 25 per cent (Kensington and Chelsea where other forms of renting accounted for 54 per cent of households). House prices in Greater London and the South East of England are the highest in Britain and this spatial polarisation of housing tenure is associated with a broader pattern of social segregation. The inner London boroughs include the major concentration of economic, social and housing stress. In a recent analysis based on 1981 Census data and creating standardised scores to provide a single index of deprivation, only two of the 19 outer London boroughs had basic scores in excess of any of the 13 inner boroughs (excluding the City of London). Only three of the outer London boroughs but all of the inner London boroughs (excluding the City of London) had over ten per cent unemployment.

Against this background the progress of council house sales, especially under legislation providing council tenants with a right to buy, has had a clear impact. In the period 1974-1978 relatively few council house sales were completed. The decision to sell or not was at the discretion of the local authority and discounts to encourage tenants to buy were less generous than under the legislation of 1980. Only three inner London boroughs sold over 100 dwellings in this period and five outer London boroughs sold none. Sales clearly were not reducing tenure differences in this period. However, it is the much higher rate of sales after 1978 which represents the most striking restructuring of housing tenure. In the period 1979 to 1982 over 54,000 council dwellings were sold in Greater London. Over the same period some 73,000 new dwellings were completed; only 15,000 of these were in the private sector and 51,000 were new council houses. Yet in Greater London as a whole council housing was in absolute decline and its privatisation through sales to tenants was more significant in the growth of home ownership than the activities of speculative housebuilders. Between April 1979 and December 1982 almost three quarters of all sales were in the outer periphery. There is a clear relationship between sales and low rates of unemployment and urban stress. In inner London only the City of London, with a very small public housing stock, and Wandsworth are among the high sellers. Wandsworth's position is principally the result of a local policy to sell vacant council dwellings in addition to sales to sitting tenants.

It is clear that the pattern of disposal of public sector dwellings is sharpening tenure polarisation between inner and outer London. If we take account of claims from tenants to buy (as opposed to completed transactions) the pattern is the same. Changes in the geography of tenure in London is likely to continue to reinforce established differences. Two final points should be mentioned in this connection. First, council flats and maisonettes have been heavily under-represented amongst sales. This applies in both inner and outer London boroughs and implies a greater coincidence between tenure and dwelling type throughout London. However, these dwelling types are most heavily represented in inner boroughs. Second, council dwellings are sold at prices related to a market valuation. Even with discounts of up to 60 per cent available to tenants, this places sale prices in excess of what many sitting tenants can afford. Evidence from inner London (Hackney) and outer London (Hounslow) suggests that income and occupation factors are important in determining who buys, and comparisons with less high priced regions indicate that these factors are more important in determining the social and spatial pattern of sales in London than they are elsewhere (Forrest and Murie, 1984a). Again this reinforces the inner-outer polarisation but it also implies a tenure polarisation within individual boroughs throughout London.

Liverpool

In Liverpool local spatial data on social malaise can be linked with tenure. It demonstrates the concentration of the marginal poor in parts of the council stock and the inner city. Tenure transfers associated with council house sales tend to reinforce rather than break down these links. In the period since 1961 there has been a net loss of manufacturing employment in Liverpool. In addition, there has been a decline in port-related and associated industries located around the docks and city centre, and a movement of new manufacturing industry and some established firms to peripheral areas where good environmental conditions were combined with modern housing, new industrial estates and access to the national motorway network.

The decline in employment in city centre areas has only partly been balanced by the growth of services. The growth of such services was not as significant in Liverpool as in similar commercial centres elsewhere in the country or in the competing Manchester conurbation. In any case this employment was not on the whole of a suitable type for those laid off from declining sectors. The impact of changes in the structure of employment in the city centre on workers living in these areas was particularly great because of difficulties in travelling to work to locations where jobs were to be found. Car ownership was low, and the travel time and fares involved in travel to the new employment growth centres were very high (Nabarro, 1980). The 1981 Census indicates that dependency on public transport remains high in the inner areas. In some areas 90 per cent of households are reliant on the public network of services.

As everywhere, the continuing rise in unemployment has hit some groups more than others. School leavers, the unskilled and ethnic minorities are particularly affected. Other groups which generally fare badly in the labour market (young people with a poor work record, ex-prisoners and the long-term unemployed) fare particularly badly in Liverpool. In a declining labour market those who have jobs hold on to them and there is a lower turnover in jobs that tend to be characterised by a high turnover under other circumstances. Employers, with a greater degree of choice in recruiting, discriminate against blacks and those with varied and inconsistent work records (even where the jobs involved are seasonal or traditionally involve breaks in work) and offer few apprenticeships. The employment service, faced with such a large number of unskilled workers seeking employment, tends to give more help to those who will find it easiest to get work - the skilled and those who have completed an apprenticeship or attended a government training centre - and to provide training opportunities to the best qualified (Nabarro, 1980).

The households experiencing this labour market trap, in which those with least skills and most labour market 'impediments' are pushed to the bottom, are particularly those living in inner city areas, although it is also evident in other areas including some of the post-war peripheral council estates (Nabarro, 1980). Outmigration, clearance, disinvestment and the concentration of the poorest sectors of the working class have created a striking coincidence of physical decay and social disadvantage in Liverpool's inner area. Drawing on data from the city's planning department, it is possible to link a number of variables with areas of low status housing in general and public housing in particular.

When variables commonly associated with disadvantage (large families, single parenthood, car ownership, overcrowding, unemployment, black households, unskilled employment, junior clerical or manual employment) are mapped at ward level, predominantly rented areas tend to score high on a larger number of variables than other areas. This is not a feature only of areas consisting predominantly of council housing. Indeed, inner areas of mixed public and private renting are in the highest percentage group for more variables than any other wards. What is marked, however, is that areas with higher percentages of owner occupation are less likely to fall into the highest percentage groups on the variables selected. The two variables where this pattern is most consistently broken are single parent families and ethnicity, and these variables (especially ethnicity) are those most seriously affected by sampling error.

This can be elaborated using cluster analysis. Liverpool City Council has created 128 basic data zones (BDZs) which are as far as possible internally homogeneous. The 128 BDZs are grouped into 24 clusters, twelve of which contain a significant level of local authority accommodation. From these, six 'neighbourhood types' have been identified which provide a general perspective on differentiation in council housing. These range from medium status areas to very low status areas.

Areas of private rented housing and of council housing are differentiated not only in terms of age, type and location of dwellings but in their social characteristics. The areas of lowest status housing coincide with the areas of highest unemployment. While these differences would be expected to affect the pattern of privatisation of public housing, the association between council house sales and social and economic malaise is also crucial in terms of who benefits from sales and in terms of the impact of sales on those trapped in different parts of the housing and labour market.

The sale of public sector dwellings, which forms part of the general strategy of privatisation, exacerbates the relationship between marginalisation in housing consumption and marginalisation from the labour market. Typically, the process works selectively, benefiting those in the best public sector dwellings, those in the strongest bargaining position and those in skilled manual occupations. What is presented as a process which liberates the public tenant from the bureaucratic paternalism of state welfare has precisely the opposite effect on those who remain. Processes of segregation and stigmatisation are accentuated.

Schemes for the disposal of public dwellings have operated in Liverpool at various times since 1962, although the details of policy have changed. Over ten per cent of dwellings were sold in 16 BDZs and of these only four were within the inner city area. Of the 35 BDZs where over five per cent of the council stock was sold, only six were within this inner city area. The pattern of sales tends to reinforce a division between areas of rented housing (public and private) in the inner city on the one hand, and some peripheral estates and areas of owner occupation on the other. Areas which are themselves, or are next to, areas of relatively high home ownership are becoming more exclusively owner occupied, and this is a more striking feature than the trickle of owner occupation into largely rented areas. For those continuing to rent, the spatial distribution and quality of accommodation available to rent is becoming more limited.

The pattern of disposal of publicly owned dwellings can be compared with the council housing neighbourhoods referred to earlier. What emerges (Table 2.2) is a general trend for sales to be highest in highest status areas and minimal in lower status areas.

Table 2.2: Council Housing Neighbourhoods in Liverpool

	Disposals as a proportion of stock of dwellings 1971–1981 %
Medium status	9.2
Low status	5.4
Low status recently built inner area	0.9
Low status recently built outer area	1.3
Very low status predominantly council	Nil
Very low status mixed rented	0.5

The three areas with over 1,000 council dwellings where no disposals occurred between 1971 and 1981 are in the central area where levels of home ownership are very low. The predominantly council areas with high rates of disposal are, with one exception, those areas which exhibit least evidence of social stress. The current drive to accelerate the rate of disposal will further consolidate these trends.

A more up-to-date analysis based on housing management districts can be made. Liverpool is divided into seven districts for housing management purposes. The North and South City Districts comprise the redeveloped inner city areas around the docks where over 80 per cent of council dwellings are flats. In the other five districts fewer than one-third of council properties were flats. The pattern of lettings and transfer requests fits with a picture of the North and South city areas catering disproportionately for those with least bargaining power in the allocation process. Against this background the pattern of sales and applications to purchase under the right to buy, taken in conjunction with evidence on the stock and patterns of activity over the last ten years, indicate that the geography of council housing in Liverpool is being substantially changed. Its concentration in inner city areas and flats is becoming more pronounced. Those sections of the population with least ability to purchase in the market and with least bargaining power in negotiating access to council housing will have fewer alternatives to housing in these inner city areas. The links between economic circumstances, tenure, dwelling type and location will become more pronounced. Those in a labour market trap are in an increasingly tight housing trap as the supply of properties available to transfer out of the inner city declines. Those able to buy are experiencing an increase in opportunities to move - to starter homes or resold council houses. But those in the labour market trap are unable to spring their escape from the housing trap.

The implications of this pattern are of an increasingly polarised and segregated city. The areas of the city are sharply differentiated in both housing and employment terms, and increasingly the housing and employment patterns are coinciding. Areas where economic stress is greatest are least affected by the growth of owner occupation. If present trends continue the more affluent council housing areas will increasingly become owner occupied. Council housing will be more distinct in its design and spatial distribution and the operation of the housing market will more firmly damage the position of council tenants in the labour market and other situations. Council house sales become a major element in sharpening tenure polarisation.

There are other factors which add to the problems of inner city residents who are disadvantaged in the employment market. They are affected by inconvenient location in relation to job opportunities, by reduced opportunities for renting outside the inner area, and arguably, by a hardening of images and social reputation associated with area of residence as disadvantage is increasingly concentrated. However, the impact of high rents, increasing dependence on means-tested housing benefit and the poverty trap provide the final element tying employment and the housing situation into a circular mesh of mutually reinforcing disadvantages; these exclude those living in certain areas from a variety of opportunities and privileges available to others.

CONCLUSIONS

The relationship between changes in state housing and economic stress in London and Liverpool displays certain similarities. There is an inner and outer area polarisation and an increasing coincidence between economic status and housing tenure. There are also similarities associated with the relative importance of flats and maisonettes in the council stock, their concentration in inner redeveloped areas and their under-representation among council house sales. However, there are important differences. In Liverpool council housing is highly represented in outer areas and its relatively faster rate of sale is crucial. In London polarisation was already marked through differential new building rates and a long tradition of territorial defence (Young and Kramer, 1978) and high house prices. In Liverpool building for sale and local authority support for owner occupation have been the major factors in the recent growth of home ownership, although the coincidence of high land prices on the edge of the city and local authority plans to build for sale in the inner city have suited the building industry (Grosskurth, 1982). Liverpool has a large stock of older terraced properties in inner city areas, and priced well below the cost of new building. In this context neither council house sales nor build for sale schemes offer a source of lower priced accommodation. There is already a low priced market for lower earning households to buy in the inner city. The key factors in tenure polarisation and social segregation operate in a different way than in London, but they produce as clear a pattern, and one as strongly linked to economic and social stress.

The coincidence of these patterns in urban concentrations such as London or Liverpool should not be too much of a surprise, but neither should it lead to a neglect of more diffuse and complex interrelationships. This evidence is consistent with tenure polarisation, but it is not adequately summed up by the concept, and it also draws attention to other issues. Tenure polarisation in some cities appears to be a phase in social polarisation, and too exclusive a focus on it would lead to a neglect of other elements in social polarisation, including division between disadvantaged and advantaged forms of owner occupation. A recognition of tenure polarisation must not blind us to other dimensions of inequality. Indeed, inequalities in wealth and capital accumulation, and continuities in housing between generations merit attention and should not be lost sight of against a background of aggregate trends in tenure.

Tenure polarisation may be increased by current policies such as council house sales but its origins lie in the organisation of housing and in longer term patterns of building, finance and control. The changing structure of tenure is currently taking place against a' background of economic recession. The growth of a large section of the population who are peripheral to the labour market is an important element in understanding changes in housing.

For example, state housing in Britain is often regarded as having developed as a means of reproducing labour power or as an ideological concession designed to control or fragment class conflict. However, as economic recession fragments the working class, its potential for organised political action declines and its maintenance can be achieved at reduced cost to the fiscal system. As council housing becomes more uniformly second class housing, so stronger links with income and economic position will emerge. The associations between second best housing and poverty would be reasserted and council housing, rather than breaking the link between low income and poor housing, would become part of that link. However, diversity within other tenures would mean that council housing was by no means the exclusive link. The public sector has been a major route to better housing conditions. It has more recently been a major route - through council house sales - to owner occupation. Policy changes could of course change its role or composition. The conversion of council housing as a whole to owner occupation would remove tenure polarisation and the current association between tenure and household characteristics. It would not remove the elements of social inequality and social polarisation which have become identifiable with tenure. It would merely mean that differences within tenures would need greater attention. If only for this kind of reason it is important to see tenure polarisation in the context of social polarisation and differentiation within tenures. The evidence from aggregate data is much more relevant in this context and it is supported by studies in particular localities taking into account the considerable variations in the meanings of tenure in different areas and at different periods. Both tenure and social polarisation are appropriate and useful shorthands to convey a picture of increasing inequality between social groups and geographical areas. If social polarisation implies a wider canvass and the sense that crucial processes in tenure division are not only housing processes, it is a necessary part of any discussion of tenure polarisation. But just as important, it is necessary to move beyond a conceptualisation of social change in terms of two poles. Reference is needed to segmentation and differentiation and to the issues of power and social participation which enable explanations of change to be offered and which account for changes in the lifestyles and life chances of particular groups.

Chapter Three

THE RESIDUALISATION OF COUNCIL HOUSING IN INNER LONDON
1971-1981

Chris Hamnett and Bill Randolph

INTRODUCTION

        For 60 years, from 1919, to 1979, the British
housing scene was characterised by the continued if uneven
expansion of both owner occupation and council housing. Since
1979, however, the sitution has changed dramatically. With
the election of a radical right government committed to
'rolling back the frontiers of the state' and the creation of
a mass 'property owning democracy', the continued expansion
of the council sector has been stopped dead in its tracks and
thrown into sharp reverse. Since 1979 central government
expenditure on council housing has been cut by over half, new
council building has collapsed to its lowest peacetime level
for 60 years, council rents have been raised sharply and,
since the government introduced its right-to-buy legislation
in 1980, some 900,000 council houses have been sold to
sitting tenants at considerable discounts.
        The current attack on council housing is without
doubt the most fundamental and severe reversal suffered by
the sector in a long history of advances and retreats, and,
not surprisingly, the last few years have also been marked by
a growing concern over the extent to which the role and
status of council housing in Britain is being reduced to a
residual welfare housing tenure catering increasingly for the
economically and socially marginalised. As Murie (1982,
p.34) has commented:

        the late 1970s and early 1980s are an important
        watershed in policy. The developments imply
        more than just a speeding up of existing
        trends. They also imply more than simply a new
        period of retrenchment and concentration on
        special needs. They imply a new era for council
        housing ... which ... involves a reassertion of
        the role of the market backed by a minimal poor
        law service.

But, whilst Murie is correct to argue that these developments represent a fundamental departure from previous policies and not just a speeding up of existing trends, neither the trends nor the debate over the future of council housing are solely a product of the last five years. The rapid growth of the council sector during the 1950s and 1960s levelled off during the 1970s and the proportion of council tenants increased only marginally between 1970 and 1980. Thus, although residualisation can be seen as 'part and parcel of the general reorientation in state intervention towards the facilitation of market processes and away from direct provision ... these processes were established well before the current phase in policy' (Forrest and Murie, 1983, p.465).

RESIDUALISATION IN CONTEXT

The 'residualisation debate' may have been triggered off by the Conservatives' desire to cut back council housing in favour of owner occupation but it cannot be attributed to that alone. On the contrary, as Harloe (1978a, 1981) and others have argued, there has been a general tendency since the beginnings of the current world economic crisis in the early 1970s for housing and other services previously provided by the state in advanced capitalist economies to be 'reprivatised', or 'recommodified', as part of a general strategy to 'recapitalise capitalism' and cut the burden of state welfare expenditures. These tendencies have been well documented in a variety of countries (Harloe and Martens, 1985), and it should not be forgotten that the cuts in British housing expenditure in 1976 in the aftermath of a financial crisis were made by a Labour chancellor.

Crucial as these changes have been, there is a good case to be argued that they represent the latest stage in a much longer process of tenurial and social change which has been taking place over the last 60 years or more. A number of separate arguments can be identified. Kemeny (1981) has suggested that the growth of both owner occupation and the council sector throughout the post-war era in Britain was only made possible by the sale into owner occupation of large numbers of privately rented properties. As the supply of such properties begins to dry up, the continued growth of owner occupation becomes increasingly reliant upon either, or both, the cutting back of new council building or the sale for owner occupation of council dwellings. To the extent that Kemeny is correct, the introduction of the right-to-buy legislation was an obvious policy option for a radical right government committed to the expansion of a mass 'property owning democracy'. By simultaneously reducing the size of the state sector and increasing the level of owner occupation, council house sales kill two birds with one stone.

Kemeny is not alone in stressing the importance of long-term changes in the structure of housing tenure. A number of other commentators (Hamnett, 1984; Malpass, 1983; Murie and Forrest, 1980) have emphasized the link between the residualisation of council housing, the wider process of socio-tenurial polarisation and the changing structure of tenure provision. The general thesis runs as follows. Up until the first world war, the privately rented sector — which accounted for some 90 per cent of all households - was socially heterogeneous. During the 1920s and 1930s, however, skilled manual workers were increasingly housed in the growing council sector whilst better off white-collar workers moved into the expanding owner occupied sector. During the post-war period these tendencies continued but, as it continued to expand, owner occupation attracted an increasing number of skilled manual workers from both the council and the privately rented sectors. Simultaneously, the council sector began to accommodate a growing proportion of the less skilled, the poor, the elderly, and various ethnic and social minorities previously concentrated in the declining privately rented sector. The result of this tenurial restructuring of the housing market is that the population has become increasingly socially differentiated between the two dominant tenures.

The 'socio-tenurial polarisation' thesis outlined above tends to stress the role of changes in structure of housing tenure as though they occurred in isolation. This is clearly not the case and more recently Ball (1982), Forrest and Murie (1983) and Hamnett and Randolph (1986) have all emphasised the relationship between changes in the labour market and changes in the housing market. While owner occupation has become a differentiated mass tenure, those groups who have been marginalised in the labour market are becoming more and more concentrated in the council sector. Ball (1982) goes further to argue that the growing concentration of the economically active and more highly skilled in the owner occupied sector is paralleled by a shift in the structure of government subsidies away from council housing and towards owner occupation.

The tendencies towards socio-tenurial polarisation and the association between marginalisation in the labour market and the housing market, are seen primarily as products of changes in the structure of housing tenure over the last 25 years. But at least three authors - Harloe (1981), Murie (1982) and Saunders (1984) - have suggested that the decline of the council sector from a 'mass' to a 'residual' role is part of a longer term transformation in the structure of housing provision in Britain. As Murie (1982, p.35) has put it:

It is reasonable to argue that since the last half of the nineteenth century a fundamental change has occurred in the way in which housing has been consumed. In the nineteenth century the most appropriate mechanism for financing housing production and consumption was private landlordism, but for various reasons this has changed. Individual private ownership (owner occupation) has emerged as the most apppropriate mechanism in the twentieth century. But the period of transition and transfer ... involved particular strains and shortages which (through political action) have been offset by state intervention ... By the 1980s it is arguable that the period of transition is over. The transitional role of council housing is therefore being abandoned and its permanent role is a more limited one.

Murie's analysis is a convincing one, but why should this transition from private renting to owner occupation have come about? Like Saunders, Harloe (1981, p. 30) argues that, given the high price of housing in relation to incomes and the consequent necessity for most buyers to borrow a large sum and repay it over a long period of years, mass owner occupation:

only emerges when substantial proportions of the potential consumers have stable long-term earnings; and this only occurs when there is a reasonable approximation to the conditions of long term growth and freedom from unemployment accompanied by rising real incomes, which was generally apparent after the second world war, and in some circumstances began to emerge in the interwar years.

Despite their differences, all the theses outlined above have one thing in common - an emphasis on the changing role of the council sector. But in their paper on residualisation and council housing, Forrest and Murie (1983) were at pains to argue that residualisation is a multi-dimensional process which is seen to involve economic, political, ideological and social dimensions. They also argue that, although residualisation affects the council sector most severely, it is neither tenure specific nor related solely to changes in the housing market. On the contrary, they argue that residualisation is the product both of changes in state policies towards welfare and housing provision, and of changes in the structure of the labour market which are economically marginalising certain sections of the working class, as well as of changes in tenure structure generally. Taken collectively these processes are resulting in the concentration of the economically marginalised in both the council tenure and, to a lesser extent, in low income marginal owner occupation.

To the extent that 'residualisation' can be argued to involve a variety of different processes which have operated differentially over both time and space, any attempt to quantify the extent of residualisation is fraught with problems. The first point which it is necessary to make is that there can be no one unitary measure of residualisation. Any measure can only be a measure of one aspect of the various residualising processes at work. But as Malpass (1983, p. 44) has pointed out:

> Despite the diversity of ways in which residual is used it is clear that the common theme running through them is the idea of local authority housing as a narrow welfare tenure, confined to the poor people and people with special needs. The most important criterion in the definition of a residual public sector is the social composition of the tenants, and it is generally understood that a residualised municipal housing service would be largely, if not completely confined to those amongst the low paid, the unemployed, the elderly, single parents, the disabled and others who were so disadvantaged in the housing market that they were unable to obtain adequate accommodation privately.

Up until the present, the 'residualisation debate' has been understandably concerned with attempts to describe and analyse the nature of the residualisation process in general terms. There have been relatively few attempts to delineate empirically the scale and extent of what can be termed the 'social residualisation' of council housing and the wider process of socio-tenurial polarisation of which it is a part (Hamnett, 1984; Robinson and O'Sullivan, 1983). In the rest of this chapter the focus is therefore on the analytical and measurement problems associated with social residualisation of council housing at the local level.

THE MEASUREMENT OF POLARISATION AND SOCIAL RESIDUALISATION

If the theorisation and definition of social residualisation presents a major problem, the measurement of its incidence and extent is almost as difficult. There are problems over the choice of variables, data availability, and scale and comparability over time. Given what has been said above regarding the growing concentration of the less skilled, the unemployed, the elderly, the economically inactive, the poor, and various disadvantaged social and ethnic minorities in council housing, the measurement of social residualisation could in theory be carried out using a variety of indicators. In practice, however, there are a number of problems regarding the availability and the geographical scale of disaggregation of some indicators which inhibit analysis. If we ignore one-off surveys which are both expensive and of limited comparative utility, we are effectively presented with a choice between the use of government survey data and the census of population on the one hand, and the analysis of tenant records on the other.

The analysis of tenant records is potentially an extremely valuable research tool at the local authority level, not least because it can be used to analyse the changing social composition of individual estates. It can also be linked to an analysis of allocation rules and procedures. But, while it is possible to monitor changes in the characteristics of new tenants alone, it requires the analysis of both incoming and outgoing tenants over a period of time in order to be fully effective. It is also likely to prove extremely time consuming and labour intensive unless a computerised record system is established. On the other hand, government social surveys such as the General Household Survey and the Family Expenditure Survey are readily available and both allow differences in income, socio-economic group and household type to be examined across tenures, while the availability of income data is a clear advantage over the census (Robinson and O'Sullivan, 1983). Both are, however, national surveys and the sample size makes the examination of differences at the sub-national level very problematic. The General Household Survey has also only been carried out since 1971 which makes the examination of long-term changes difficult. It does, however, have the advantage of being carried out annually unlike the census. This means that the impact of policy and other changes on the social composition of the different tenures can be more closely monitored.

The principal advantage of the decennial census of population is that it can be used to monitor changes at a wide variety of geographical scales from the national to the local authority and even the enumeration district. But the census is not without its problems. One problem of using published census data as an indicator of socio-tenurial polarisation or residualisation is that the majority of variables tabulated by tenure relate to number of rooms, persons per room, household amenities and the like. Many of the more potentially interesting variables are simply not disaggregated by tenure, certainly not at the sub-regional scale. Even where such tables are available they are not always available from one census to another. Thus, although the 1981 Census includes an extremely valuable small area table showing the socio-economic group (SEG) of heads of household by tenure, the only previously published table giving this information is for England and Wales as a whole in 1961 and by standard regions in 1966. No published tables of SEG by tenure were available from the 1971 Census.

The amount of longitudinal analysis that can be done using published SEG by tenure tables from the census is therefore rather limited. Changes in the distribution of SEG by tenure can be carried out for England and Wales for the period 1961-1981 with the addition of some 1971 data from the Housing Policy Review (Department of the Environment, 1977) and this has already been carried out (Hamnett, 1984). It is also possible to examine changes from 1966-1981 on a regional basis. This has been done for Greater London (Hamnett, 1983a) and work is in hand on the changing tenurial and socio-economic structure of the housing market in London and the South East. The main findings of the national analysis of changes in SEG by tenure are summarised below.

SOCIO-TENURIAL POLARISATION IN ENGLAND AND WALES 1961-71-81

In the 15 years from 1945 to 1961 the tenurial structure of the housing market in England and Wales changed dramatically. Whereas the privately rented sector was still the largest sector with 62 per cent of households in 1945, it had declined to second place with 33 per cent by 1961. The proportion of owner occupiers rose from 25 to 43 per cent and council renting doubled from twelve to 24 per cent. By 1961 owner occupation had already diffused quite widely down the socio-economic hierarchy although, not surprisingly, the structure of diffusion was clearly socially specific. Although 67 per cent of professional and managerial household heads were owner occupiers, the proportion fell systematically to just 22 per cent of unskilled heads. In the council sector the pattern was reversed, rising from seven per cent of professional and managerial heads to 39 per cent of unskilled heads (see Table 3.1). Lest it be thought that the unskilled dominated the council sector, and the professional and managerial groups the owner-occupied sector, at this time, it should be stated that these figures ignore the size of the different socio-economic groups. In 1961 skilled manual workers were by far the largest group in the council sector where they accounted for 42 per cent of households, the semi-skilled accounting for a further 23 per cent. Collectively, therefore, these two groups accounted for two out of every three households.

By 1981 the virtual collapse of the privately rented sector and its replacement by what are now the two main tenures had both changed and reinforced these socio-tenurial distinctions. Although owner occupation accounted for no less than 83 per cent of professional and managerial households and 70 per cent of intermediate and junior non-manual households, it had also become, at 58 per cent, the majority tenure of skilled manual workers. But although owner occupation had diffused even more widely down the socio-economic hierarchy by 1981, its diffusion was still socially uneven. In the three highest socio-economic groups

Council Housing in Inner London

owner occupation increased by between 15 and 18 percentage
points from 1961 to 1981. Amongst the unskilled it grew by
only nine percentage points and amongst the economically
inactive it remained static.

These differences are more clearly brought out when
we look at the council sector. In both the non-manual
groups the proportion of households in council housing
decreased from 1961 to 1981. Amongst skilled manual
households it grew by only two percentage points over the 20
year period (and all the increase was in the 1960s; in the
1970s the proportion actually fell by three points). Among
semi-skilled and unskilled households the proportion of
council tenants increased by ten and 17 percentage points
respectively, and amongst the economically inactive the
proportion increased by no less than 25 percentage points.

The overall picture is clear. Whilst owner
occupation has percolated progressively further down the
socio-economic hierarchy, it has done so in a very uneven
manner. Meanwhile, council housing has increasingly become
the tenure of those unable, by reason of occupation, income
or other circumstances, to enter owner occupation. Whereas
skilled manual workers have moved into owner occupation, the
semi-skilled, the unskilled and the economically inactive
have moved into the council sector. The socially
heterogeneous privately rented sector has been replaced by
owner occupation for the more skilled, and by council tenancy
for the less skilled and the economically inactive. By 1981
the economically inactive were level pegging with skilled
manual households as the largest groups of council tenants in
absolute terms. Whilst the decline of the privately rented
sector and its replacement by owner occupation and council
renting have resulted in the wider diffusion of owner
occupation right down the socio-economic scale, it has also
resulted in a growing differentiation between the skilled
manual and non-manual groups on the one hand and the
semi-skilled, unskilled and economically inactive on the
other. The growth of council renting and owner occupation
since 1945 has been accompanied not by the withering away of
socio-tenurial polarisation but by its intensification. Much
the same is true of the changes which took place in Greater
London from 1966 to 1981 (Hamnett, 1983). The problem
remains, however, of how the analysis of residualisation can
be carried out at the local level given the paucity of
socio-economic and other data disaggregated by tenure. This
issue is taken up below in the context of a study of social
residualisation we have carried out for inner London between
1971 and 1981.

POLARISATION AND RESIDUALISATION IN INNER LONDON

Methodology
The lack of socio-economic and other data

39

Table 3.1: Socio-Economic Groups by Tenure and Head of Households, England and Wales, 1961, 1971 and 1981

		Owner Occupiers		Council Tenants		Other	
		%	ppc	%	ppc	%	ppc
Professionals, Employers and Managers	1961	67.3	+ 8.5	6.8	+ 0.9	25.9	- 9.4
	1971	75.8	+ 6.9	7.7	- 1.2	16.5	- 5.7
	1981	82.7	+15.4	6.5	- 0.3	10.8	-15.1
Intermediate and Junior Non-Manual	1961	53.4	+ 5.9	15.3	+ 2.7	31.3	- 8.6
	1971	59.3	+11.2	18.0	+ 2.9	22.7	- 8.3
	1981	70.5	+17.1	15.1	- 0.2	14.4	-16.9
Skilled Manual and Own Account Non-Professional	1961	40.0	+ 7.8	29.3	+ 5.1	30.7	-12.9
	1971	47.8	+10.6	34.4	- 3.1	17.8	- 7.5
	1981	58.4	+18.4	31.3	+ 2.0	10.3	-20.4
Semi-Skilled Manual and Personal Service	1961	28.7	+ 7.9	32.3	+ 6.9	39.0	-13.8
	1971	35.6	+ 6.0	39.2	+ 2.7	25.2	- 8.7
	1981	41.6	+13.9	41.9	+ 9.6	16.5	-22.5
Unskilled Manual	1961	21.9	+ 5.1	38.9	+10.4	39.2	-15.5
	1971	27.0	+ 3.9	49.3	+ 6.6	23.7	-10.5
	1981	30.9	+ 9.0	55.9	+17.0	13.2	-26.0

Table 3.1 (Contd.)

		Owner Occupiers		Council Tenants		Other	
		%	ppc	%	ppc	%	ppc
Students and Not Stated	1961 1971	42.3	+ 0.1	17.1	+24.9	40.6	-25.0
Economically Inactive	1981	42.4		42.0		15.6	
All Socio-Economic Groups	1961	43.1	+ 7.3	23.6	+ 4.4	33.3	-11.7
	1971	50.4	+ 7.3	28.0	+ 0.8	21.6	- 8.1
	1981	57.7	+14.6	28.8	+ 5.2	13.5	-19.8

Note: The first column for each tenure refers to the percentages of households in that tenure in each year. The second column refers to percentage point changes; the first and second figures give ppc for 1961-71 and 1971-81 respectively, and the third figure the overall ppc for 1961-81.

Sources: 1961: 1961 Census, England and Wales, Household Composition Tables, Table 4
         1971: Housing Policy Technical Volume, Part I, HMSO, 1977, Table II.28.
         1981: 1981 Census, England and Wales, 10% Sample, Table 49.

disaggregated by tenure on a small area basis is not a new problem, but this study attempts to circumvent the difficulty by developing the methodology first employed by the Runnymeade Trust (1975) in its study Race and Council Housing in London. The trust set out to investigate the proportion of households of New Commonwealth origin in GLC housing, and the location, type and quality of their accommodation. In the absence of data on country of birth by tenure, the trust conceived the novel idea of identifying a number of council estates large enough to comprise one or more complete enumeration districts (EDs) in the 1971 Census. This was achieved by matching up large-scale ED boundary maps with maps showing the distribution of GLC housing estates. Having then isolated all those EDs with more than 95 per cent local authority tenants, it then proved a relatively easy matter to analyse the racial composition of these estates by simply reading off the number and proportion of household heads born in the New Commonwealth or Pakistan from the relevant ED tables. As a result, the trust were able to show convincingly that racial minorities were disproportionately over-represented in many of the older, poorer, inferior flatted estates in inner London, and under-represented in the better and more desirable suburban cottage estates. What the trust researchers did by isolating council estates in this way was effectively to hold tenure constant. Consequently, they were able to treat the data on country of birth as tenure specific.

Clearly, this methodology is not limited to the examination of data on race. It can be used for the whole range of variables given in the ward library data for identifiable estates which comprise one or more complete EDs. It can also be used to measure change over time, provided that the ED boundaries of existing estates remain the same. The social characteristics of new estates (those built after one census but before the next) can also be analysed and compared with the composition of existing estates. This methodology is not restricted solely to the analysis of large council estates. It can also be used to examine the changing social composition of EDs comprised exclusively of privately rented or owner occupied housing. The present authors have also previously employed this methodology to analyse the changing social composition, tenure and vacancy levels in the purpose built flat sector in central London by identifying 101 large blocks of private purpose built flats which comprised separate EDs in both 1971 and 1981 (Hamnett and Randolph, 1983b).

In the research which we report here the methodology was used to analyse the changing social composition of all those council estates in the London boroughs of Lambeth and Camden which had the same ED boundaries in both 1971 and 1981. Whilst this approach clearly excludes the analysis of that part of the council

sector not found in such estates, the insights it affords
outweigh its limitations. There is also the problem that
other tenures are excluded from the analysis. In effect we
are able to look at only one side of the polarisation coin.
We can, however, attempt to measure the extent to which large
council estates can be said to have become increasingly
'residualised' in terms of their social composition vis-a-vis
the boroughs as a whole. Before looking at the results of
this analysis it is necessary to set the work in context by
briefly examining the changing tenure structure of the
housing market in both inner London as a whole and the study
boroughs.

The Tenurial Transformation of Inner London 1961-1981

The 20 years from 1961 to 1981 have seen a complete
tenurial transfórmation of inner London. In 1961 almost
two-thirds (64 per cent) of all households rented privately,
and the council and owner occupied tenures accounted for only
19 and 17 per cent of households respectively. As late as
1971 almost one in two (49 per cent) households still rented
privately, whilst council renting had increased to 30 per
cent and owner occupation to 19 per cent. The rapid growth
of council renting at the expense of the private rented
sector was already well established in the 1960s, and the
1970s saw the continuation of this trend. By 1981 only 30
per cent of households still rented privately (half the 1961
figure) whilst the proportion of council tenants and owner
occupiers had increased to 43 and 27 per cent respectively.
Council tenure was the largest tenure in 1981. For a more
detailed analysis of the changing tenure structure of Greater
London's housing market see Hamnett and Randolph (1983a).

Social Residualisation in Lambeth and Camden

Both Camden and Lambeth approximate quite closely
to these overall changes. Between 1971 and 1981, the period
covered by our study, the number of households in both
boroughs fell by almost 15 per cent. The losses were
concentrated in the privately rented sector, which declined
from 48 to 30 per cent of all households in Lambeth and from
60 to 37 per cent in Camden. Both the council and
owner-occupied tenures experienced absolute increases. The
number of council households in Lambeth increased by 7,000 or
20 per cent and the proportion of such households rose from
31 to 43 per cent. In Camden the number of council
households increased by 7,500 or 38 per cent and the
proportion rose from 24 to 39 per cent. Owner occupation in
Lambeth increased from 20 to 27 per cent and in Camden from
14 to 24 per cent. Council renting in both boroughs now
comprises a much larger slice of a smaller pie.

The local authority housing estates which formed
comparable EDs in 1971 and 1981 accounted for almost half
(47.5 per cent) of all local authority households in the two

43

Table 3.2: Changing Socio-Economic Composition of Household Heads in Camden and Lambeth, 1971 and 1981

		Group 1		Group 2		Total	
Comparable Local Authority EDs	1971	964	33.8%	1892	66.2%	2856	100%
	1981	757	28.7%	1876	71.3%	2633	100%
Borough Totals	1971	8098	42.0%	11191	58.0%	19289	100%
	1981	6878	41.5%	9692	58.5%	16570	100%
LAA EDS as % of Borough Totals	1971		11.9%		16.9%		14.81%
	1981		11.0%		19.4%		15.89%
Ratio of LAA% to Borough %	1971		0.80%		1.14%		
	1981		0.69%		1.22%		

Source: 1971 and 1981 Censuses, unpublished small area statistics.

boroughs in 1971. By 1981 the total number of households in these EDs had fallen by 2,500 or 8.7 per cent, and they comprised just over a third (36 per cent) of all council households in the boroughs. This is the result of the continued expansion of the local authority sector. The range of variables available for examination was limited by both definitional changes and comparability problems, but the variables we eventually chose for analysis were selected to provide as wide a measure of social residualisation as possible. They included the SEG of both economically active and retired heads of household, the SEG of economically active and employed persons, the economic activity status of persons by sex, persons born in the New Commonwealth and Pakistan, and pensioner households. In the analysis which follows we have chosen to concentrate on just four variables for ease of presentation.

Changes in Socio-Economic Composition

There has been a growing trend throughout the seventies for council housing to be the tenure for those excluded from owner occupation, either because they are too old to embark on the mortgage cycle or because they cannot afford it ... It is quite likely that owner occupation is now the majority tenure for the 'economically active' sectors of the working class. (Ball, 1982, p.63).

Council housing, by contrast, is thought to be accommodating the economically inactive and the economically marginalised. In order to examine the validity of this thesis in Lambeth and Camden we have aggregated all the data on the SEG of heads of household into two categories. The first category comprises all those household heads classified as managerial, professional, intermediate non-manual, non-professional self-employed and own account workers, and skilled manual workers. The second category comprises all household heads classified as junior non-manual, semi-skilled and personal service workers, the unskilled, the inadequately described and the economically inactive. The results are shown in Table 3.2 and they clearly support Ball's thesis. Whereas in the comparable local authority areas (LAAs) a third of all household heads were in the first category in 1971, their proportionate share fell by five percentage points to 28.7 per cent in 1981. Conversely, the proportionate share of the second category increased from 66 to 71 per cent. By contrast, in the two boroughs as a whole, the share taken by each of the categories remained virtually constant over the intercensal decade at 42 and 58 per cent respectively. When the local authority estate figures are excluded from the borough wide figures the contrast is even sharper.

The changes in the socio-economic composition of
the local authority sector compared to the other tenures are
revealing but the extent of residualisation cannot be
quantifed simply in terms of occupational group data as
Robinson and O'Sullivan's (1983) work clearly indicates. We
therefore examined changes in a number of other variables.

Changes in the Economic Activity Status of Resident Persons
The late 1970s saw a dramatic rise in the level of
unemployment. In order to assess the extent to which the
unemployed and the economically inactive became increasingly
concentrated in the council sector, we examined the changing
numbers and proportions of the economically active, inactive
and unemployed in the local authority estates in Camden and
Lambeth between 1971 and 1981, and compared these to changes
in the boroughs as a whole. Looking first at the
economically active in employment, the figures in Table 3.3.
show that, compared to the boroughs as a whole, the LAAs were
characterised in both years by lower proportions of male and
female economically active and employed persons. The
proportion of unemployed males and females in the LAAs was
also consistently higher than in the boroughs as a whole.
This is hardly surprising. The significance of the results
lies in the differential nature of the changes. The
proportion of economically active and employed males in the
LAAs fell from 36.4 per cent of the total population aged 16
years or over in 1971 to 28.8 per cent in 1981, compared to a
fall from 36.6 to 31.7 per cent in the boroughs as a whole.
Similar, though slightly less marked, changes occurred where
the proportions of economically active and employed females
were concerned.

The growth of unemployment in the LAAs was very
marked. In 1971 unemployment in the LAAs was 6.5 per cent
of the economically active population, compared to 5.8 per
cent in the boroughs as a whole. In 1981 unemployment had
risen to 18.5 per cent in the LAAs and 12 per cent in the
boroughs as a whole. The number of unemployed males and
females in the LAAs rose between 1971 and 1981 by 104 and 62
per cent respectively compared to rises of 78 and 43 per cent
in the boroughs as a whole. As a result, the proportion of
the total number of unemployed persons in the two boroughs
who were resident in the LAAs increased from 17.8 per cent in
1971 to 20.3 per cent in 1981. Given the significant amount
of double counting involved in comparing changes in the LAAs
to changes in the boroughs as a whole (which include the LAA
figures), it is clear that if the changes in the LAAs could
be compared to changes in either the non-LAA areas or the
other tenures, the differences would be even more marked.

Council Housing in Inner London

Table 3.3:   Economic Activity and Unemployment in Camden and
             Lambeth, 1971 and 1981.

	LAA EDs		Boroughs	
	1971	1981	1971	1981
	%	%	%	%
Males, economically active and employed	36.4	28.8	36.6	31.7
Females, economically active and employed	27.6	24.0	27.8	26.0
Males, economically active and unemployed	2.8	6.6	2.4	5.2
Females, economically active and unemployed	1.7	3.1	1.6	2.7
Males, economically inactive	6.8	10.4	7.4	9.9
Females, economically inactive	24.7	27.0	24.1	24.5

Note: Data relate to persons aged 16 and over.

Source: 1971 and 1981 Censuses, unpublished small area
         statistics.

        This point also applies to the changing proportions
of the economically inactive in the LAAs. Here again, the
economically inactive not only comprised a higher proportion
of the population of the LAAs than they did of the boroughs
as a whole in both time periods, but their degree of
over-representation actually increased over time. Whereas
the economically inactive in the LAAs in 1971 comprised 15.9
per cent of the total number of the inactive in the borough,
this figure had risen to 17.8 per cent in 1981. Given that
the size of the council sector increased considerably in both
boroughs over this period, it is reasonable to surmise that
the proportion of the economically inactive population
accounted for by the local authority sector as a whole
increased by considerably more. This is certainly the case
nationally.
        When we look at the changing proportions of the
unemployed and the economically inactive taken together, it
is clear that the LAAs experienced a disproportionate
increase in relation to the boroughs as a whole. Whereas
these groups accounted for 36 per cent of the total LAA
population aged 16 or over in 1971 compared to 35.5 per cent
in the boroughs as a whole, by 1981 the proportions had

increased to 47.1 and 42.3 per cent respectively. This is
an increase of 11.1 per cent in the LAAs compared to 7.8 per
cent in the boroughs as a whole. When the extent of double
counting in the borough wide figures is allowed for, the
difference would be greater still. Overall it is clear that
the economically active and employed have become increasingly
concentrated in the LAAs in Lambeth and Camden and, we
suspect, in the council sector as a whole in these boroughs.

The Changing Concentration of New Commonwealth Immigrants and the Retired

In the late 1960s and 1970s numerous articles and
reports appeared which drew attention to the low proportion
of new commonwealth immigrants in the council sector relative
to their numbers in the population as a whole. This
under-representation was attributed, amongst other things, to
the impact of residence qualifications and allocation systems
which awarded 'points' for years on the waiting list, both of
which de facto discriminated against new arrivals
irrespective of active discrimination. Subsequently,
however, an increasing proportion of both British born blacks
and new commonwealth immigrants have found their way into the
council sector. This is particularly true of West Indians,
and table 11 of the Housing and Households volume of the 1981
census shows that, whilst 24 per cent of all households in
England and Wales with a head born in the New Commonwealth
and Pakistan were council tenants in 1981, the figure varied
from 45 per cent of heads born in the Caribbean to 13 per
cent of heads born in India. Although the increasing
proportion of blacks in the council sector could be
interpreted as a welcome opening up of the sector, it can
also be seen as indirect evidence of growing residualisation,
given the generally disadvantaged position of these groups in
the housing market.

Such caveats aside, the analysis of intercensal
change reveals some very clear changes. Whereas the number
of persons in the two boroughs as a whole who were born in
the New Commonwealth or Pakistan remained constant at around
47,000, the number living in the local authority estates
increased by 75 per cent, from 4,800 to 8,400 (Table 3.4). As
a proportion of the total number of persons in the LAAs they
almost doubled from 6.6 to 12.8 per cent. In the boroughs
as a whole the proportion rose from 9.8 to 12.2 per cent. So,
whereas persons born in the New Commonwealth or Pakistan were
under-represented in the LAAs in 1971 compared to the
boroughs as a whole, they were very marginally
over-represented by 1981. To the extent that the doubling
of the proportion of blacks in council housing is a
reflection of both their disadvantaged housing market
position and the out-migration of whites into owner
occupation it can be interpreted as prima facie evidence of
residualisation.

Table 3.4: Concentration of Persons born in the New Commonwealth and Pakistan, and Pensioner Households, in Camden and Lambeth, 1971 and 1981

	LAA EDs			Boroughs		
	1971	1981	Change	1971	1981	Change
Persons born in New Commonwealth and Pakistan	4809	8438	+75.5%	47433	47653	+ 0.5%
As % of all Persons	6.0%	12.8%		9.8%	12.2%	
Pensioner Households	6013	6676	+11.0%	39022	38331	- 1.8%
As % of all Households	21.1%	25.6%		20.1%	23.1%	

Source: 1971 and 1981 Censuses, unpublished small area statistics

The last variable to be considered here is that of pensioner households. Such households have increased dramatically over the last 20 years, from seven per cent of all households in England and Wales in 1961 to 14 per cent in 1981 (Office of Population Censuses and Surveys, 1984). As Table 3.4 shows the proportion of pensioner households was 50 per cent higher in Camden and Lambeth than it was nationally (see Warnes and Law, 1984 for a detailed analysis of the changing distribution of the elderly). The most significant feature is not that the proportion of pensioner households was slightly higher in the LAAs than it was in the boroughs as a whole, but that the number of pensioner households in the LAAs increased by eleven per cent compared to a decrease of almost two per cent in the boroughs as a whole. By 1981 pensioner households were far more concentrated in the LAA sector than they were in 1971.

CONCLUSIONS

We have not concerned ourselves in this chapter with the actual mechanisms and processes which have underpinned and intensified the degree of socio-tenurial polarisation in Britain over the last 20 years (see Hamnett, 1984 for a discussion of this topic). It is therefore impossible to say how far the changes discussed above reflect changes in the structure of housing opportunities and constraints and how far they reflect changes in the structure of the labour market. This is a subject for debate. What is clear from the Lambeth and Camden evidence is that the council sector has indeed become increasingly socially residualised during the 1970s. Whether we look at income, socio-economic group, economic activity or unemployment, it is apparent that the council sector now accommodates a higher proportion of the economically marginal than it did in 1971. The rapid increase in unemployment since the 1981 Census, and the effects of the changes in government policy towards the council sector compared with owner occupation, are likely to intensify these tendencies. Whether by accident or design council housing is increasingly being pushed into the role of welfare safety net for the economically and socially marginalised. To the extent that these trends reflect conscious policy decisions to reduce the attractions of council housing they are likely to set in chain a circular and cumulative process of socio-tenurial polarisation whereby all those able to afford to enter owner occupation do so and where council housing becomes increasingly the preserve of the poor, the unemployed, the elderly and the desperate.

Chapter Four

THE FINANCIAL ASPECTS OF CHANGE

David McCulloch

INTRODUCTION

This chapter examines the framework of financial assistance to the public sector in England. In so doing it concentrates largely on local authorities, where most change has taken place. The starting point for the analysis is the election of the Conservative administration in 1979. This is deliberate as it is since then that there has been a substantial shift in the volume and emphasis of the financial support given to public sector housing. Reductions were imposed before 1979 by the preceding Labour administration, particularly on capital spending limits; these, however, were much more limited in their effects.

The chapter, therefore, sets out to explain events since 1979. It is not an economic appraisal or an assessment of the balance of financial advantages between tenures. Rather, it attempts to illustrate the direct and indirect pressures which have been brought to bear on the public sector as part of the government's stated intention to make local authority housing self-financing and to promote further growth of owner occupation through the sale of council houses. By examining the measures that have been taken so far, along with ministerial and other statements, it is suggested that the effect of current policies, taken to their logical end, will be the creation of a 'residual' public sector occupied by low income households living in the remaining, lower quality, local authority stock. In arriving at that conclusion consideration is given to the main forces affecting public expenditure on local authority housing between 1979/80 and 1984/85.

The general framework for local authority housing finance is outlined, followed by specific accounts of the arrangements for capital expenditure and control, housing revenue account (HRA) subsidies, rate fund contributions and rents. Each of these sections then goes on to consider the changes that have occurred over the period and, where appropriate, their effects. The remaining sections review the shift in the approach of central government to housing that has taken place, and the likely future position of the public sector, particularly the local authority sector, should present policies continue.

Reference is made throughout this chapter to housing 'subsidies'. There is considerable debate as to what constitutes a subsidy, particularly amongst those who compare the relative financial advantages of owner occupation and public renting. In this respect economists are likely to see matters differently from, say, administrators or political scientists. The analysis here is not so much concerned with these relative advantages as with the effects on the local authority sector, and on local authority tenants, of the change from direct to the indirect assistance which has been introduced since 1979. Essentially what has happened is that assistance to the public sector has moved from direct subsidy, through exchequer grant and rate fund contributions to the HRA (and rate support grant paid towards the latter), to indirect assistance through the means-tested housing benefit system.

There are, however, difficulties in quantifying the predecessors to housing benefit before the scheme was introduced in 1983. Prior to the creation of housing benefit, means-tested assistance with housing costs was divided between the rent and rate rebate and rent allowance schemes, and the housing element in supplementary benefit. It is not easy to bring together information from these various schemes in such a way that the data would be directly comparable with that for housing benefit. For the purposes of this chapter, therefore, references to means-tested assistance are restricted to the period following the introduction of housing benefit.

Scotland and Wales are not included for a number of reasons. Scotland, with its different legislation, and political and administrative arrangements, would merit a chapter of its own, although the end result of rent policy is very similar to England. Wales has parallel legislation to England but the course of events and arguments put forward differ to some extent. Again, the end result of recent policy is similar in effect.

PUBLIC EXPENDITURE AND LOCAL AUTHORITY HOUSING FINANCE

The construction, repair, maintenance and administration of council housing is funded partly by central government, partly by local government and partly by the tenant. Central government, through the Department of the Environment (DOE), approves borrowing by means of the housing investment programme (HIP) system to allow certain capital expenditure to take place. It provides direct subsidies to help offset loan charges on the money borrowed, it subsidises routine management and maintenance expenditure, and it allows, through the rate support grant (RSG), limited assistance to local authorities for 'essential' rate fund contributions to the HRA. At the level of the individual tenant it provides assistance with rent through housing benefit for those with resources sufficiently low to qualify. Approximately 65 per cent of local authority tenants are currently in receipt of assistance with either rent or rates through housing benefit.

A local authority may meet part of the costs of its housing through making a contribution from the rates to the HRA. Certain rate fund contributions are in fact statutory. But many HRAs are now in surplus and there is often a subsidy the other way, from the HRA to the rate fund. However, in inner city authorities rate fund contributions may still be very substantial.

The tenant pays for housing through rent and, indirectly where a rate fund contribution is made, through rates. Central government capital allocations and assistance for revenue spending are determined on an annual basis, and they are tied in with the public expenditure planning process.

Capital Expenditure

English local authorities receive borrowing limits from government through the HIP system. Capital expenditure on housing encompasses new building, improvement and capitalised repairs to council housing, slum clearance, house renovation grants, lending to housing associations and mortgages. The present capital control arrangements were set up under the Local Government, Planning and Land Act, 1980 while the HIP system, which preceded this act, was incorporated into the arrangements.

Authorities have considerable freedom, in theory, with the capital allocations they receive, whether they are for housing or other spending areas. For instance, housing allocations can be swapped in full with those for other purposes, such as personal social services or education, and ten per cent of an authority's overall borrowing limit can be rolled forward into the next year. Borrowing for housing purposes can be increased by the addition of 20 per cent of local capital receipts from sales of houses and land. This percentage has been steadily reduced, in an effort to control expenditure, from 50 per cent in 1981/82 to its present level.

Table ·4.1 shows HIP allocations and capital expenditure between 1979/80 and 1984/85. The figures have been repriced in constant price terms to allow for inflation.

Table 4.1: HIP Allocations and Capital Expenditure

	HIP Allocation (£m)[1]	Gross Expenditure (£m)[1]
1979/80	4,160 (original)	
1979/80	4,097 (revised)[2]	4,175
1980/81	2,938	3,006
1981/82	2,252	2,417
1982/83	2,067	2,645
1983/84	1,894	3,087
1984/85	1,853	3,200[3]

Notes: [1] At estimated 1984/85 outturn prices.

[2] The revision from £4,160 million to £4,097 million was made by the incoming Conservative government.

[3] Estimate.

Sources: The Government's Expenditure Plans, 1985/86 to 1987/88, Cmnd. 9428, HMSO, 1985; earlier public expenditure white papers; and DOE annual HIP announcements.

Prior to 1981/82 local authorities were not permitted to increase their borrowing to take account of capital receipts; the receipts were 'taken up' nationally and redistributed through the HIP mechanism. To some extent this explains the drop in allocations between 1980/81 and 1981/82, although, clearly, the largest fall took place in 1980/81. This was a result of direct government cutbacks. It also explains why gross expenditure in later years exceeds the reducing HIP allocations, as authorities gradually increased expenditure through the use of accumulated capital receipts. Overall, direct HIP allocations over the period fell by 60 per cent, although when allowances are made for separate government assumptions on the amount of receipts expected to be generated locally, the reduction is in the region of 46 per cent. The most significant reduction, 36 per cent in one year, took place between 1979/80 and 1980/81 and was followed by a spending freeze in late 1980 until the end of the financial year. This took place because the relevant cash limit was under threat.

The 1980/81 moratorium had a marked effect on local authority confidence which, in combination with expected HIP reductions for 1981/82, made that year a low point for expenditure. With the introduction of the new arrangements for capital receipts from the April 1981, local authorities found themselves with the ability to extend their spending by 50 per cent of accumulated receipts. This did not show up through increased spending until 1982/83.

In the autumn of 1982 the government announced what was virtually a free-for-all on capital expenditure. Receipts from council house sales had accumulated much faster than they were being spent, and there had been considerable lobbying from the construction industry and others at the beginning of the lead-in to the 1983 general election. Partly as a result of this green light, and partly as there had been a general gearing up of spending anyway, capital expenditure increased markedly in 1983/84 to £3,087 million. It would have been much higher for 1984/85 had the government not announced a policy of 'voluntary restraint', essentially a moratorium, in July 1984 to protect the relevant cash limit.

After the general election in June 1983 curbs on spending were increased, starting with an end to temporary higher levels of private sector improvement grants in October 1983. Five hundred million pounds was then taken out of the 1984/85 housing programme as a whole through the Chancellor's 1983 autumn statement, and the proportion of receipts added to local expenditure limits was reduced from 50 per cent to 40 per cent. The ten per cent difference was incorporated into the national HIP, allowing a reasonable allocation to be made in comparison to the previous year. Despite these national cutbacks individual local authorities continued to expand their programmes within the limits of available resources, as they were legally entitled to, and had, indeed, been strongly encouraged to do in the autumn of 1982 by both the Prime Minister and the then Secretary of State for the Environment, Michael Heseltine.

The Group of Eight, a standing body of contractors' organisations, professional bodies and construction trade unions met the Prime Minister in early October 1982. Shortly after this Mrs Thatcher wrote to the local authority associations urging that councils increase their capital spending through the use of receipts. A series of meetings took place between the DOE, local authorities and the construction industry, the first one being chaired by the Secretary of State. The object of these meetings was to increase local authority capital spending.

Not only have there been considerable direct cutbacks in the capital programme; there have also been restrictions on the purposes for which resources could be spent. For instance, early in the government's first term of office, purchase of properties from the private sector, 'municipalisation', was virtually stopped. Local authorities were discouraged from holding land banks through measures such as the Land Register and new subsidy arrangements. It became, and still is, very difficult for local authorities to purchase land for general needs public sector housebuilding purposes.

The effect of these reductions in spending and the redirection of priorities has been very considerable. Surveys carried out by the Association of Metropolitan Authorities, the Institute of Housing and others show deferment of repair and modernisation programmes, delay of work to put right unsatisfactory systems built housing and shelved new build schemes, including elderly and disabled persons' accommodation (Association of Metropolitan Authorities, 1982a and 1983; Institute of Housing, 1984).

On the capital expenditure side, therefore, there have been considerable changes in the arrangements for, and level of, spending in the public sector. Local authority housing has been considered secondary to the need to control and reduce public expenditure. The stop, go, stop, year-by-year policies have caused considerable frustration and loss of confidence by housing authorities in the planning of longer term programmes. Housing has continued in its role as an economic regulator but, over the past years, local authority housing has suffered the most of any public expenditure programme.

Housing associations have also been affected, particularly in the level of funding from local authorities. In real terms this fell by 57 per cent between 1979/80 and 1984/85 (Great Britain, 1985). However, Housing Corporation funds to associations have remained more or less constant over the period. Overall, the voluntary sector has been cut back on capital funding but not to the same extent as local authorities.

LOCAL AUTHORITY HOUSING SUBSIDIES

The current local authority housing subsidy system for England was introduced in 1981/82. It is a deficit based system designed to pay subsidy on the basis of centrally assessed deficits on local authority HRAs. Authorities are expected to make a 'local contribution' to HRA income which is determined on an annual basis. Subsidies are adjusted each year to take account of the gap between local contributions and outgoings which, in theory, an authority can make up either through rents or rate fund contributions. In practice, changes in local contributions are equivalent to the level of rent increase the government expects to be made in that year; an increased rate fund contribution is extremely difficult to achieve in the present climate of RSG penalties and rate capping.

There are three main components of the present housing subsidy system:

Base Amount (BA) which is the starting point for subsidy in any year and consists of existing entitlement to subsidy from previous years.

56

<u>Housing Costs Differential (HCD)</u> which is the loan charges arising from new capital expenditure during the year in question.   It also includes a set increase in the allowance for management and maintenance expenditure.

<u>Local Contribution Differential (LCD)</u> which is decided on an annual basis by the Secretary of State and is basically his assumption of the amount by which local authorities should raise rents during the year.   For 1981/82 the local contribution differential was £2.95 per dwelling per week, and for 1982/83 it was £2.50.   Each local authority's housing subsidy entitlement is adjusted downwards to take account of this 'contribution'.
    Actual subsidy entitlement is the Base Amount (what the local authority is getting already) plus the Housing Costs Differential (to take account of increased expenditure) minus the Local Contribution Differential (assumed rent increase).   In other words, subsidy entitlement equals BA + (HCD - LCD).   If an authority's increase in expenditure (HCD) is more than it will put back in to the system through its local contribution (LCD) subsidy entitlement goes up;   if the opposite is the case subsidy entitlement will be reduced.
    As will become clear in the later sections of this chapter, subsidies have been reduced to such an extent that the government's version of the overall national HRA is in profit, with only very few local authorities still receiving subsidy.

Table 4.2 : Housing Subsidy

	£m[1]
1979/80	2,050
1980/81	1,900
1981/82	1,142
1982/83	559
1983/84	295
1984/85	360[2]

Notes: [1] At estimated 1984/85 outturn prices.
        [2] Estimate.

Source: <u>The Government's Expenditure Plans 1985/86 to 1987/88</u>, Cmnd. 9428, HMSO, 1985.

    Subsidies to local authority housing were reduced by approximately 85 per cent in real terms between 1979/80 and 1983/84 (Table 4.2).   The greatest reductions took place in 1981/82 and 1982/83, the years when the government required the largest increase in local contributions.   The fall in interest rates over the period has also reduced the subsidy total to some extent.

Rate Support Grant and Rate Fund Contributions

Housing is included in RSG to take account of those elements of rate fund contributions to the HRA (for those authorities making contributions) which the government accept as necessary. RSG itself is made up of a series of a grant related expenditure assessments (GREAs), of which one is carried out for housing to reflect the revenue effects of rate fund contributions to the HRA. The method used to arrive at the annual GREA for housing involves the projection forward of a national 'notional' HRA constructed by the DOE. The HRA model used for this purpose, known as LOCHRA, is constructed from individual HRAs for all authorities in England. In producing this national HRA, assumptions are made on rents, management and maintenance expenditure, inflation, council house sales and other items (McCulloch, 1981). The procedure sets the control total or cash limit for this element of the RSG calculation.

The method to distribute these resources is by a complex formula known as 'E7' (McCulloch, 1981). The method involved is a considerable over-simplification of the factors affecting HRAs and was intended as a temporary measure until an alternative could be formulated. Penalties are built in to the system for higher spending authorities which make rate fund contributions to their HRA yet have rents lower than the regional average and for authorities with higher than average voids.

As the national model assumes authorities to be following government guidelines, most councils are now assumed to be in surplus on their HRA and they no longer receive assistance through this part of RSG. In theory this should mean that these authorities would have their RSG reduced to take account of notional surpluses, and indeed this happened in 1981/82. However, the authorities affected, mainly smaller district councils, lobbied ministers both individually and through their local authority association, the Association of District Councils (Association of Metropolitan Authorities, 1982b). The lobbying was successful and at the very last moment before the announcement of 1982/83 allocations the arrangements were changed. Authorities with notional HRA surpluses were allowed to keep them without affecting their RSG position. In other words, notional surpluses are no longer clawed back and RSG entitlement is unaffected; this concession has become known as the 'zero option'.

The main consequence of the zero option is that little pressure can be brought to bear on rent levels through this route for authorities in notional surplus. However, the financial penalties for authorities with high cost and continuing subsidy entitlement – essentially those in London – still remain. These authorities are still in an HRA deficit position, and both their subsidy and RSG are reduced annually to take account of assumed increases in local contributions (in effect rent increases).

Table 4.3 sets out the housing GRE position from 1981/82 to 1984/85 and compares it with what would have been the position if the zero option had not been introduced. It also lists actual rate fund contributions.

Table 4.3   Rate Support Grant and Rate Fund Contributions

	Housing GRE Control Total (ignoring authorities in 'surplus')	Housing GRE Control Total (taking into account authorities in 'surplus')	Actual Rate Fund Contributions
	(A)	(B)	(C)
	£m[1]	£m[1]	£m[1]
1981/82	299[2]	299	529
1982/83	358	160	477
1983/84	305	−20[3]	529
1984/85	250	−284[3]	n/a

Notes: 1   At estimated 1984/85 outturn prices.
        2   The 'zero option' did not apply in 1981/82.
        3   The negative figures indicate a surplus.

Sources: The Government's Expenditure Plans, 1985/86 to 1987/88, Cmnd. 9428, HMSO, 1985, Table 3.7; and DOE data as supplied to the English local authority associations following RSG settlements of 1982/83 to 1984/85 (repriced to estimated 1984/85 outturn).

Column A shows the rate fund contributions assumed necessary by the government to balance the notional national HRA, ignoring those authorities assumed to be in surplus (that is the zero option). Column B shows the 'true' notional HRA position, taking into account those authorities assumed to be in surplus. The differences between columns A and B reflect the zero option concession. However, as column C shows, actual rate fund contributions are running considerably above government targets. There has been much less scope for councils to increase the use of rate fund contributions to offset rent rises in recent years owing to the operation of RSG and, for some authorities, rate capping. Rents are being raised through these less direct methods as well as the direct sanction of subsidy and RSG withdrawal.   Trends in rent levels are examined below.

Council House Rents
          The legal position on local authority rent levels
is that they should be 'reasonable', and that an authority,
in setting rents, should have regard to the balance between
contributions from its ratepayers and its rent payers.
          Table 4.4 sets out the average local authority rent
levels in England between 1980/81 and 1983/84   (Column A).
Rents effectively doubled over the period.

Table 4.4: Local Authority Rents: England

	Average Weekly Rent	Average Weekly Rent if Guidelines had been followed by all authorities
	(A)	(B)
	£	£
1980/81	8.18	n/a
1981/82	11.15	11.43
1982/83	13.59	13.93
1983/84	14.03	14.78
1984/85	14.71	15.53

Source: Chartered Institute of Public Finance and
          Accountancy, Housing Rents Statistics
          (annual).

          The second column (B) sets out where rent levels
would have been if authorities had obeyed the government's
guidelines.   Clearly, the 1981/82 and 1982/83 increases were
steep compared to the following two years.   However, with
two-thirds of tenants in receipt of housing benefit, and each
rent increase pushing more into benefit, there are
diminishing returns to the government in continually pressing
for large increases.   They have to pay much of the rent
increase to local authorities through subsidy to meet the
cost of housing benefit.
          With more and more authorities no longer receiving
housing subsidy, and the zero option operating for
authorities which have run out of entitlement to assistance
through the housing element of RSG, the government has less
direct scope than previously for forcing rents up.   Without
the removal of the zero option, which may prove politically
difficult, or other penalties there is little that can be
done to remove the gap between actual rents and the levels
which the government would like to see set.

A CHANGED APPROACH TO HOUSING POLICY

The preceding analysis has demonstrated a
considerable reduction in direct subsidy to local authority
housing and its replacement by indirect assistance through
the means-tested Housing benefit system.   Direct assistance
- housing subsidies and rate fund contributions - fell by
£1,747 million in real terms between 1979/80 and 1983/84.
Expenditure on housing benefit rose over the period but a
similar comparison is not possible as the scheme changed in
structure and was affected by a rising level of
unemployment. However, at present, 3.1 million tenants in
England and Wales receive housing benefit, of whom 1.75
million have their rents and rates paid in full.   The bill
for 1984/85 is estimated to be £1,960 million.

These financial changes have been accompanied by a
very considerable shift in approach to public sector, and in
particular local authority, housing by the present
administration.   This change in approach has, it is argued,
broken any post-war consensus which may have still existed in
housing policy.   The main tenet of policy since 1979 has
been the increase of owner occupation, with a particular
emphasis on the sale of council houses.   This has been
achieved by a combination of legislative change, financial
incentives and well-organised publicity.   The Housing Act,
1980 was the legislative vehicle, giving the right to buy to
the majority of public sector tenants at discounts, which
were subsequently extended from a maximum of 50 per cent to
60 per cent of market value.   This initiative was combined
with reductions in direct assistance to local authority
housing and the rent increases described above.   The
extension of owner occupation to lower income groups has also
been encouraged through concepts such as the shared ownership
and improvement for sale.

Changes Between 1979 and 1983
During the early years of Michael Heseltine's term
as Secretary of State for the Environment, and John Stanley's
as Minister for Housing and Construction, emphasis was placed
on getting the right to buy off the ground.   The Housing
Act, 1980 assisted a rise in council house sales from 42,500
in 1979 to 207,000 in 1982.   It was during the latter part
of this period that the most substantial shifts in financial
assistance took place.

Despite their magnitude these financial changes
were introduced, largely, as 'technical' adjustments, on an
incremental basis.   With the exception of rent increases and
reductions in capital expenditure through the HIPs, they were
subject to little open debate.   Most of the debate appears
to have taken place behind closed doors, within the DOE and,
presumably, the Conservative Party.   There was certainly
very little public discussion.   Individual meetings aside,

dialogue between local authorities and the government was restricted to the twice-yearly meetings of the Housing Consultative Council, meetings between ministers and representatives of either local authorities or the local authority associations, or was lost in the generality of rate support grant debates in parliament. For example, rent increases and subsidy decreases were introduced as 'local contributions' and presented as technical or administrative changes. Mechanisms to reduce rate fund contributions were incorporated within the overall rate support grant control mechanisms and lost from the housing debate.

In 1980 the newly constituted House of Commons Environment Committee chose to examine the government's future expenditure plans for housing in the light of the severe reductions outlined in the then current public expenditure white paper (House of Commons, 1980). The white paper showed that 75 per cent of the planned reductions in public expenditure were to come from the housing budget.

The committee called before it both Michael Heseltine and John Stanley for an oral session. This session indicated the shift in housing emphasis that had begun in 1979. Although not helpful in terms of detail, ministers expressed the general direction of policy in making it clear that housing expenditure was tied in very closely with, and would be overridden by, macro-economic policies and requirements. Furthermore, future planning of housing requirements, and resources to be committed to the field, would have to proceed on a year-to-year basis according to financial circumstances and decisions related to the economy as a whole. Planning for future housing provision was considered to be unreliable and had been halted within the DOE (House of Commons, 1980). This approach went against the 'conventional wisdom' of the planning of future housing requirements introduced by the HIP system and the 1977 green paper (Great Britain, 1977). Housing need was no longer a subject for discussion; it was not on the immediate political agenda of the government. Increasingly, during this first period, discussion of 'difficult' policy areas was deflected by the government. The policy measures and their financial effects were, however, clear enough.

One arena where consultation did continue, partly as a statutory requirement, was at meetings between ministers, DOE civil servants and the local authority associations. These were mainly at the formal gatherings of the Consultative Council on Local Government Finance (CCLGF) and Housing Consultative Council (HCC). CCLGF deals mainly with rate support grant matters, including the housing element. HCC deals with most other housing matters including subsidies, rents and capital spending.

Rent policies, and the government's view on the relations between rents, subsidies and capital spending, were spelt out by Michael Heseltine at HCC meetings during this period. He argued consistently for large rent increases in order to preserve the capital programme at as high a level as possible within the overall control total for public spending on housing. There was a clear relationship in that high rents resulted in less exchequer subsidy, hence allowing a larger proportion of the total to be available for capital spending. By 1984, however, rent increases had become much less useful from this point of view owing to the low level of subsidy and the public expenditure implications of rising levels of housing benefit payments.

To a large extent the local authority associations either agreed, or at least did not disagree violently, with this approach. These matters were discussed at the autumn HCC meetings preceding the announcements on local contributions for 1981/82 and 1982/83. The Conservative controlled Association of District Councils and London Boroughs Association generally agreed the increases suggested by the Secretary of State. The Labour controlled Association of Metropolitan Authorities was generally neutral, not wishing to argue for lower rents at the expense of the capital programme. This position changed to opposition when the capital programme was cut further despite large rent increases. Understandably there was no meeting of minds on the need to reduce the overall level of housing expenditure, and ministers tended to repeat the same public expenditure arguments that had been made to the House of Commons Environment Committee.

The effective closing down of the housing debate, in particular the non-discussion of major questions of policy, continued during 1981 and 1982. Several consultative bodies were wound up or restricted in their role. For instance, John Stanley closed down the Housing Expenditure Steering Group, an official level body made up of representatives from the local authority associations and the DOE. This was the consultative forum which looked at the likely future RSG requirement for housing, arising from 'necessary' rate fund contributions, in the light of expected future expenditure, and it had been part of the public expenditure planning process. Similar groups for other services continued. A separate consultative group, dealing with GREAs for housing, was closed down at the end of 1982. Again, groups for other services continued.

By the time of the 1983 general election, the housing debate might have faded completely into the background had it not been for the results of the 1981 English House Condition Survey (DOE, 1982) and pressure on the Prime Minister from the construction industry to do something to increase capital expenditure. However, in autumn 1982, and resulting from these events, the emphasis suddenly switched to increasing capital spending. A substantial volume of capital receipts from council house sales permitted a relaxation of spending controls. Local

authorities, after three years of declining programmes, were
suddenly told to 'spend, spend, spend' on the capital
front. Councils were asked to bid for more resources in all
capital areas, not just housing. As mentioned earlier,
renovation grants received a very considerable boost and
local authorities began to draw up expansion plans which
resulted in the higher levels of outturn for 1983/84 and
1984/85. However, the capital expenditure initiative turned
out to be very short term indeed. Full clarification and
articulation of the new directions of housing policy were
only to appear after the general election and a change in
ministers at the DOE.

1983 Onwards

Following the general election, government policies
towards the local authority housing sector, and the financial
approach in particular, became more explicit. Patrick
Jenkin had taken up the post of Secretary of State and Ian
Gow that of Minster for Housing and Construction.

At the November 1983 HCC Jenkin outlined the main
points of the government's approach, which have been repeated
consistently since. The view expressed was that local
authority housing programmes should, in the future, be geared
more to special needs provision for groups such as the
elderly and disabled rather than to 'general needs'
housing. Ministers also indicated that housing subsidy
should continue to decrease through rent increases and that
they would like to see its eventual elimination. Local
authority rent levels should continue to rise, not only to
cover debt repayment, management and maintenance, but also to
reflect more closely the value of the house as an asset. The
Secretary of State was also concerned to see the cost of
council housing brought more in line with other tenures
(essentially owner occupation).

These statements of policy have been repeated on
numerous occasions since, both by ministers and senior civil
servants. Limitations on the type of new local authority
housing to be built are already being put into effect. It
has become increasingly difficult to get borrowing approval
for general needs local authority building. Ministerial
speeches and the DOE letter to local authorities accompanying
the 1985/86 HIP allocations have continued to emphasise the
policy of special needs building.

CONCLUSIONS

In strictly financial terms the logical result of
policies along these lines will be local authority housing in
financial surplus with the consequent end of the need for
both exchequer housing subsidy and 'voluntary' rate fund
contributions to the HRA. The majority of district councils
are in this position already.

If rents were to rise to a level equivalent to initial mortgage costs, then the financial argument for council tenants not buying at discount, at least in the case of houses as distinct from flats, would be very difficult to resist for those who qualified for a mortgage. A further boost has been given to the right to buy through the extension discounts and eligibility in the Housing and Building Control Act, 1984. The medium-term outlook appears to be that of a gradually decreasing local authority stock occupied predominantly by people dependent on means-tested state assistance through the housing benefit system. The public sector is moving more and more towards 'welfare' housing for those who have no choice. This situation has been reinforced by the switch in allocation patterns following the introduction of the Housing (Homeless Persons) Act, 1977, particularly in inner city areas. If the better quality stock continues to be sold, then those within, or about to enter, the council sector will tend to face a more restricted choice of housing, which will often be at high density and in flats.

There is still a considerable way to go before this position will be reached, if it ever is reached. For instance, under present arrangements, it is no longer possible to raise rents without a net increase in central government as opposed to public expenditure as the increased cost of housing benefit exceeds savings on housing subsidy. Rent guidelines were for increases of 75 pence per week for 1984/85 and 60 pence per week for 1985/86, considerable reductions on earlier years. Furthermore, the right to buy has now levelled off and the past peaks are not likely to be repeated. Only a certain proportion of people at one time either can afford to buy or want to do so, although, of course, there will always be a stream of new purchasers. More radical solutions will have to be found if owner occupation is to be extended with much rapidity by the route of individual tenure change in the local authority stock. Some of these alternatives are already being experimented with, for example through schemes such as Stockbridge Village Trust, and these are discussed in chapter 9. What is clear is that a radical realignment of financial assistance for one sector of housing has taken place and is continuing with limited debate, outside academic circles, as to its desirability or likely consequences. On the revenue side, council housing is already subsidising the rates in many authorities as a consequence of rent increases over the levels existing in 1980/81. On the capital side there has been a stop, go, stop approach, in a convoluted world of capital receipts and cash limits. Council housing is undergoing considerable change with very little consistency of method, although the general policy direction is reasonably clear.

65

The question has to be asked as to whether it is appropriate, and if so to what extent, that council tenants, one of the poorest groups in society, should subsidise ratepayers. Two-thirds may be on housing benefit, but the Department of Health and Social Security will not wish to contribute to rates support for ever more. Further, if we are to reform and restructure housing finance, should not this be by reference to all tenures so as to ensure the most productive use of available resources?

If the financial arrangements for council housing alone are to be changed, then should there not be a more consistent approach than at present, working towards clear objectives, and based upon open and full discussion? For instance, if subsidy and rate fund contribution guidelines continue to be based on local authority rent levels, should there not be a more standard approach to determining rents? 'Fair' rents might be assumed for subsidy purposes but local authorities allowed discretion locally to determine the actual rent they set. Clearly, those with rents below guidelines would have to make up the difference locally. Finally, would it not be appropriate to claw back some of the profits already being made on council housing and redistribute them to other authorities for housing purposes? The whole area of housing finance is in need of full discussion and extensive reform in order to finish the job started by the 1977 green paper. In the meantime we are moving step by step, slowly but surely, to a nation divided by tenure.

Chapter Five

PRIVATISATION, MARGINALITY AND COUNCIL HOUSING

Ray Forrest

INTRODUCTION

From what might have been seen as a rather isolated
ideological battle in the housing policy debate, or as a
simple political response to the perceived demand for home
ownership among sections of the working class, the sale of
public sector dwellings now sits within a much more
generalised debate, and within a much wider set of
theoretical arguments and constructs. This has come about
partly through the recognition that what is happening to
council housing cannot be explained and understood without
some reference to a broader literature and without an
appreciation of more fundamental processes of social and
economic change. And it has come about through the
political strategies of the Thatcher administration, where
the sale of public sector dwellings has formed the vanguard
of a thoroughgoing attempt to restructure social and economic
relations, and to transform the nature and role of the
welfare state. Council house sales are now discussed in
terms of privatisation, linking the policy to a process which
emcompasses the sale of assets such as British Telecom or
British Petroleum, of public bodies such as Companies' House,
the disposal of public land and buildings, and the hiving off
of various activities of the institutions of the welfare
state (for a fuller discussion see Heald, 1983; Whitfield,
1983). Privatisation, it seems, is now everywhere.

The right to buy, introduced as part of the Housing
Act, 1980, has resulted in the sale of over 900,000
dwellings. In social and economic terms this represents a
very significant, if not the most significant, feature of the
present government's privatisation policies. Certainly it
may be the most pervasive privatisation policy in terms of
the number of individual households affected, while, to date,
capital receipts from the sale of council houses dramatically
outweigh those from other asset sales and are an important
element in public expenditure plannning (Forrest and Murie,
1984b). Indeed, council house sales are now of comparable

significance in the growth of home ownership than to speculative housebuilding; but, despite this, achieved and projected levels of sales represent a disappointment for the government. On present policies it will certainly not raise the level of home ownership to the 80 per cent of households talked of by Conservatives during the 1983 general election. Various surveys indicate a stubborn refusal by the vast majority of tenants to be cajoled into exercising their 'rights'. A survey carried out in early 1983 found that only 12 per cent of tenants were likely to buy their present dwellings (Jowell and Airey, 1984). This is consistent with findings from the Building Societies Association (1983), and indicates that the policy will deliver progressively less cash to the Treasury. The most recent public expenditure white paper anticipates a decline in total local authority receipts from £1,725 million in 1983/84 to £1,465 million in 1984/85. If the annual rate of sales declined to, say, 60,000 this would generate only half the capital receipts of 1983/84. We are therefore likely to see greater emphasis on forms of disposal of council housing which are less dependent on the unpredictable behaviour of individuals exercising their rights. This could involve more extensive sales of whole blocks to private developers or indeed the transference of estates combined with their privatised management and maintenance (strategies which are discussed in chapter 9). Many of the pressures on the public housing sector have little to do with housing policy as such or with the benefits to the household of being in one tenure or another. They relate to fiscal imperatives, where public housing is seen as an easily available source of finance and as an area where political resistance is likely to be limited.

There are, of course, pressures which derive from a view that home ownership should be extended as a matter of principle. Such a view is usually backed up by survey evidence on tenure preference which shows an overwhelming and growing desire for home ownership. In the most recent survey 77 per cent of households stated a preference for home ownership, some 16 per cent above the current national level. This compares with only 66 per cent in a 1967 survey (Building Societies Association, 1983). A critique of the interpretation of such evidence is available elsewhere (see, for example, Merrett, 1982). It is worth noting, however, that social surveys which demonstrate a progressive increase in the demand for home ownership reflect changes in policy which have structured preferences in that direction. Far from consolidating the view that such preferences are innate or natural, they show precisely the opposite. But what is more important is the problem which this structuring of preference poses for owner occupation. What we have witnessed in the last few years is not just an attack on collective housing provision; it can be more correctly perceived as a reflection of the problems of extending owner occupation in its present form. We were promised a property owning democracy, but how is it to be achieved? Despite ever more generous discounts on valuation for council house buyers, nearly 30 per cent of the population remain as public sector tenants. An array of other low-cost schemes has made only a marginal contribution (see Forrest, Lansley and Murie, 1984), while attempts by the volume housebuilders to extend effective demand through the provision of low-quality starter homes packed with consumer durables seem more likely to damage than to enhance the reputation of home ownership.

Against this background the chapter considers some of the empirical evidence on the impact of the right to buy in England and Wales. Most of the data are from the period 1979-1982, which represents the first three years of the operation of the policy. By the end of 1982 the policy had settled down and patterns had been established. These are considered at national, regional and local levels. These sections are preceded by a brief discussion of certain theoretical debates which inform the relationships between the privatisation of council housing through individual purchase, the changing role and status of council housing, and the housing position of those social groups we might appropriately label as 'marginal'. The final section considers further the argument that council housing is becoming a marginalised form of provision, and that tenure labels are indicative of a major social division.

THE NEW DEAL: SUBSIDISED INDIVIDUALISM, MARGINALISED COLLECTIVISM

Analyses of welfare provision and, more broadly, of the distribution and consumption of goods and services focus on two inter-related processes. First, there is a view that new and significant divisions are developing in the sphere of consumption. These 'sectoral cleavages' are seen as cross-cutting traditional class boundaries and producing new forms of political alignment (Dunleavy, 1980). Such processes are particularly evident in housing. Saunders (1984, p.203), for example, suggests that:

> social and economic divisions arising out of
> onwership of key means of consumption such as
> housing are now coming to represent a new major
> fault line in British society (and perhaps in
> others too), that privatisation of welfare
> provisions is intensifying this cleavage to the
> point where sectoral alignments in regard to
> consumption may come to outweigh class alignments
> in respect of production, and that housing tenure
> remains the most important single aspect of such
> alignments because of the accumulative potential

of house ownership and the significance of private housing as an expression of personal identity and as a source of ontological security.

These emergent social divisions are related to the second key process of transformation - changes in the dominant mode of consumption. Stated simply, the traditional welfare state is being undermined and eroded and is becoming a downgraded service for a residualised or marginalised minority. In turn the mass of the population are being drawn into the market place in order to satisfy their requirements. The state collective mode is being superseded by the privatised mode of consumption. In parallel with this development much of the burden of welfare provision is being shifted back on to the domestic sphere, and predominantly on to working class women for whom private alternatives to family care for the sick, the very young and the elderly are not affordable alternatives. In this sense, privatisation involves the reassertion of both the market and the family (see Balbo, 1982 for a general corrective to the view of 'the state' or 'the market' as the key features of welfare provision).

There are two features of this emergent 'privatised' mode of consumption which are of particular significance. First, it represents part of a broader restructuring of capitalist society, and is inextricably linked to changes in the labour process (particularly technological advance), the division of labour and the nature of work itself. Second, this privatised mode is not divorced from state intervention, but, on the contrary, it is heavily dependent. This is particularly notable in housing where access to home ownership, and day-to-day costs associated with repairs and maintenance, have been increasingly subsidised in various ways through grants and tax concessions. Conversely, state housing is increasingly self-financing. We must beware, therefore, of the ideological 'loading' of the term privatisation. In housing, for example, it begs the question of the extent to which council housing was ever divorced from the market in terms of its production and financing and, of more present day significance, how far owner occupation is (or ever was) the product of the free market. It is certainly becoming more appropriate to describe home ownership as a 'socialised' form of housing provision, a form of state subsidised individualism. In some respects, therefore, in answer to the question 'what is the public sector becoming?', an appropriate reply might be that it is becoming part of owner occupation.

What we are seeing is not a disengagement of the state from the sphere of consumption but a reorientation towards individualised benefits. Such a development relates to the work of Titmuss (1958) on the social division of welfare; he recognised long ago that concepts such as 'private' and 'public' were slippery and that it was by no means clear which groups in society were more or less dependent on state subsidies. Moreover, it confronts the dominant theoretical arguments of much structural Marxism of the 1970s which tended to view the provision of collective means of consumption, in the form of the traditional welfare state, as being a necessary and ever expanding feature of advanced capitalism. As Szelenyi (1981) has noted, an over-emphasis on rigid structural relationships tended to underestimate the possibilities of capitalist alternatives to collectivist welfare provision.

The key issue raised by this division between 'privatised' and 'collective' modes of consumption is how far they represent a major new fault line in British society, as opposed to reflecting (although acting upon) more profound changes elsewhere. For example, it might be argued that the major process of transformation in advanced capitalism is the extrusion of living labour from the labour process, and the significance of workers as consumers as opposed to producers. This relates in turn to the relationship between the taxable labour force and the expanding dependent population, which is the product of demographic change and industrial restructuring and poses specific problems in the context of severe economic decline. The failure of the present government to reduce rather than merely to reorient public expenditure has derived in part from the political difficulties of significantly eroding benefits for the dependent population. But there are clear limitations to state disengagement from its underwriting activities for private production. Whether nationalised or denationalised, whether contracted out or provided through public sector labour, whether labelled public or private, the 'private' sector will continue to be heavily dependent on various forms of state subsidy and tax concessions. Equally, mass consumption of (most notably) cars and dwellings requires significant subsidy through direct public expenditure and tax concessions. These two items are pivotal in creating and sustaining a lifestyle of privatised consumption. If public expenditure is to be reduced with the least damaging effects for the symbiotic relationship between mass production and mass consumption, then the target must be those areas of state expenditure which least directly or indirectly contribute to private production or individualised consumption. In this context the terms of class compromise are clearly under revision. Those groups representative of spent or surplus labour power, marginalised from the labour market and increasingly dependent on the collective welfare state, are bearing a disproportionate burden of public expenditure reductions. Whilst the collectivist welfare state reflected both the strength of organised labour and the necessity of its reproduction, the emergence of the individualised welfare state reflects the weakening and fragmentation of trade unionism, and the need to reproduce and extend consumption power.

The major fault line in British society is between, on the one hand, those engaged in wage labour, and particularly those in the growth sectors of the economy, and, on the other, the unemployed, the working class elderly, and those working in low paid and declining sectors. The divisions in consumption are themselves significant, and most notably in housing, but they are subsidiary to this bifurcation. Whilst, for those in work, living standards have generally continued to rise, the unemployed have experienced a decline in real person disposable incomes.

There are strong connections at present between council housing and the politically, socially and economically marginalised. For example, more than half the households with unemployed heads are in council housing (Office of Population Censuses and Surveys, 1984). A recent study found two-thirds of the long-term unemployed in the tenure (White, 1983). Indicators such as single parenthood and retirement can also be used to demonstrate similar associations (Forrest and Murie, 1983).

In parallel, owner occupier status has enabled households to participate, albeit differentially, in the norm of individualised, credit-based consumption. Johnson (1984) has shown that 'The current British recovery ... has been based on consumer spending increases directly attributable to the surge both in consumer credit and in home mortgages, which finance consumers indirectly'. Furthermore, the ratio of household debt to income has risen significantly, from 40 per cent in 1970 to 60 per cent in 1983, and is expected to rise further (Johnson, 1984). Much of this indebtedness, whilst attributed to house purchase or improvement and attracting tax relief of around £3 billion in 1983, leaks into other forms of consumption (Bank of England, 1982; Kemeny and Thomas, 1984). On the one hand, therefore, we have the image of the immiserated, marginalised tenant peripheral to the labour market, and of subsidised, individualised consumption by owners. But, on the other, there is the emerging image of the indebted owner, bearing a burden of credit commitments which will vary in its severity according to income. It may be clear who is relatively privileged but the question of who is or is not being exploited is a matter of some debate.

It is within this context that the sale of council dwellings takes on particular significance. The reduction in the size of the public housing sector and the reduced subsidy are the most visible part of the current restructuring of the welfare state. The provisions associated with the right to buy not only represent a major new subsidy to encourage home ownership but are part of a broader shift in the dominant mode of consumption. The transformation of the tenure structure is restructuring the pattern of housing choices, opportunities and standards, and these changes are legitimate concerns for analysis. But their significance may be underestimated unless they are related to the changing relationship between collective welfare provision and capital accumulation, and to changes affecting the nature and status of work itself. Offe (1984, p.285), for example, offers a scenario of:

> a bifurcated society organised around a shrinking capitalist core and an expanding periphery of non-market institutional arrangements and conditions of life. Within the productive capitalist core, workers will be relatively privileged. Fewer and fewer workers - mainly those who are full-employed, skilled, male and domestic (i.e. non-foreign) - will get higher and higher wages. Within the peripheries, by contrast, the old and the young, women, foreigners and mentally or physically handicapped people will become increasingly marginalised and, so to speak, accommodated by institutions other than labour markets.

Such an image of the future may seem overdramatic, and it would certainly be misleading to equate council housing too closely with this peripheral population. Nevertheless, these processes form part of the explanation of what is happening to housing provision in Britain. The important point is that the coincidence of these processes with tenure is spatially uneven and historically specific. In the final section of the chapter these relationships will be explored to demonstrate that marginality is not necessarily coincident with council housing, and that the future pattern of sales will not be a simple extrapolation of current trends.

THE CHANGING GEOGRAPHY OF COUNCIL HOUSING: THE NATIONAL AND REGIONAL PICTURE

That disposal of publicly owned dwellings has been in the forefront of the government's privatisation strategies is not surprising, given the significant part council housing has played in the British welfare state. In 1980 almost a third of all households in Britain were in the council sector, representing one of the highest levels of direct state provision of housing outside state-socialist societies. For the first time since its inception council housing in Britain is declining in both relative and absolute terms. Those unable to enter the private housing market through purchasing their council house face less choice, lower quality and higher prices for their council housing. Whilst increasingly generous subsidies are directed at owner occupation, the marginalised working class take on a higher proportion of their own housing costs. The rents of council houses increased by more than twice the rate of inflation between 1979 and 1982, while cash from the sale of council houses has been used to cushion major cuts in new housing investment and subsidy, and to allow a general reorientation of public expenditure.

The introduction of a statutory sales policy has had a major impact on the pattern of housing provision. Until the mid-1960s the number of dwellings sold by local authorities under their then discretionary powers fluctuated at fewer than 4,000 a year. Whilst the current policy can be linked to this pioneering phase, the essential difference is that until the end of the 1970s new building for the public sector far outstripped the rate of disposal. The level of sales being achieved under central government dictat bears no relation to that achieved when local government was able to exercise discretion. As Table 5.1 demonstrates, the earlier phases of high council house sales coincided with relatively high rates of new building. Even in 1973, when new building in England and Wales fell below 80,000, the council sector was still growing although low levels of construction coincided with high levels of sales. It is this relationship rather than disposals as such which is contributing to a major transformation in council housing. But the early 1980s mark a watershed in the nature of housing provision.

Table 5.1: Sales of Dwellings and New Dwellings Completed by Local Authorities in England and Wales, 1969-83

	All Sales of Dwellings	New Dwellings Completed
1969	8,590	132,634
1970	6,816	125,456
1971	17,214	107,817
1972	45,878	86,479
1973	34,334	72,388
1974	4,657	89,196
1975	2,723	110,735
1976	5,793	112,028
1977	13,020	108,483
1978	30,045	87,799
1979	41,115	69,734
1980	80,575	71,223
1981	101,905	49,411
1982	200,990	30,859
1983	144,635	30,104

Note: Sales refer to full ownership sales and exclude sales under shared ownership arrangements.
Source: Housing and Construction Statistics, HMSO.

This general contraction of the council housing
sector at the national levels conceals significant regional
variations. Prior to the introduction of the right to buy
and in the initial period of its operation, sales were
heavily concentrated in the South East region and only a very
small percentage of all sales were in the Northern region.
The impact of the right to buy has been to achieve a more
even spread of sales between regions. However, some regions
still have a disproportionately high share of sales (the East
Midlands, East Anglia, Wales and, in particular, the South
East region excluding Greater London), and others have a
disproportionately low share of sales (the North, Yorkshire
and Humberside, Greater London, the West Midlands and North
West). When these features are compared with the proportion
of council housing in each region, it is clear that the
highest sales are in those regions where council housing is
least common. The current phase of selling is thus
contributing to a greater unevenness in the form of housing
provision rather than contributing towards a convergence.
Crudely, there is emerging a regional polarisation of tenure
which has a strong North-South dimension.

If one examines the 25 localities which achieved the
highest level of sales between 1979 and 1982 (expressed as a
proportion of the publicy owned stock), none is in the North
or West Midlands, and there is a striking clustering around
the edge of London and especially in its northern and eastern
periphery. This concentration, spreading into East Anglia,
is indicated by nine of the 25 authorities being in the
Eastern region and four in the South East. Whilst council
housing is heavily concentrated in Inner London, not one
inner London borough is among the highest sellers (see
Forrest and Murie, 1984a for further discussion).

Sales have in fact proceeded most rapidly in
comfortable, affluent, less urbanised areas on the edges of
cities. They are proceeding less rapidly in those areas
usually referred to in discussion of inner city deprivation
or stigmatised council housing and in areas where the
existing rates of home ownership are lowest. The pattern of
disposal, after three years of policy implementation, was
highly selective, and this selectivity is most noticeable in
the more highly urbanised areas. Hamnett (1983b) has noted
an increasing differentiation in the Greater London area with
a growth of suburban owner occupation contrasting with an
inner core of public and private renting. A significant
feature of this pattern, evident in other cities such as
Liverpool or Birmingham, is the virtual absence of high rise
flats among dwellings sold. Whilst flats account for some
33 per cent of dwellings in England and Wales, they have
accounted for under three per cent of all council house
sales. The period of high rise building for public renting
in Britain is symbolic of a particular period of downgrading
of council housing. The selective nature of sales is

75

contributing, therefore, not only to a greater contrast between dwelling types in the owner-occupied as opposed to the council housing sector, but is accentuating the social distance between the two tenures.

THE LOCAL DIMENSION TO THE PATTERN AND MEANING OF COUNCIL HOUSE SALES

Variations in the age composition and the size and type of dwellings reflect not only different phases in the historical development of council housing but also different local social and economic structures. Council housing, council house sales and owner occupation are all categories which conceal a variety of experiences and circumstances. The varying level of sales in different areas both reflects and acts upon these substantial contrasts in the form and function of council housing. The case studies below illustrate some of these aspects.

Hyndburn, in the North West of England, which includes towns such as Accrington, has a higher than average level of owner occupation (just below 80 per cent), an ageing housing stock, low house prices and particularly severe problems of decay and maintenance. The relatively small council housing sector contains dwellings which are more spacious and of better quality than much of the existing owner-occupied stock. Many smaller, older owner-occupied dwellings lack gardens. Some dwellings command a market price of as little as £3,000. In simple terms, therefore, the image of owner occupation and council housing in Hyndburn contrasts markedly with the dominant image of suburban affluent home ownership and inner city high rise council housing. Moreover, with four-fifths of households already in owner occupation it is difficult to construct an argument regarding the frustrated desires of the local population for purchase. Indeed, the home ownership rate is above the expressed preferences for purchase for the population as a whole reported in the Building Societies Association survey (BSA, 1983).

Hackney, on the other hand, is a classic inner city area where high house prices co-exist with chronically high levels of poverty and deprivation. The council stock is dominated by high rise flats with a smaller stock of acquired and converted dwellings.

Derwentside, in the North East of England, has high levels of unemployment in Consett and adjacent towns. How does localised recession affect the owner occupied market in general and the propensity for council house purchase in particular? The issues here revolve around the potential use of redundancy payments, mobility, house price movements and the day-to-day costs of owner occupation.

Carrick, in the South West of England, is typical of a resort and retirement area under pressure from immigration. It has a higher than average level of elderly owner occupiers and its council housing sector performs a crucial role in catering for local family housing and sustaining village communities. Truro and Falmouth are the major settlements in the area. Whilst Truro displays the trappings of middle class gentrifiction, Falmouth, which contains most of the high rise council housing has suffered the effects of economic recession through the closure of the dockyards.

New Forest, which is another small rural authority, contrasts with Carrick in that it is both a commuter region for the Southampton area and a popular area for the retired. Sales of council housing in the area have been high, reflecting a stock of relatively high quality houses located on small village estates.

Hounslow is a relatively prosperous outer London borough on the western M4 corridor. Its affluence is reflected in high house prices and lower than average unemployment. Heathrow Airport and its satellite services are dominant employers with a highly unionised workforce enjoying higher than average earnings.

The information in Table 5.2 provides a general profile of tenure patterns, relative unemployment rates for males and the characteristics of the council stock. Within the six case study areas the level of owner occupation varies from 78 per cent in Hyndburn to 16.5 per cent in Hackney. Only in Hackney and (marginally) Derwentside does renting, publicly or privately, still predominate. The historical development of working class housing has been subject to considerable variation. In Derwentside 97 per cent of the stock consists of houses and bungalows. The provision of houses by employers such as the British Steel Corporation has influenced the structure of the council stock. In contrast, the position is almost the reverse in Hackney where 83 per cent of the stock is flats. Both are areas which have suffered severe impacts of the recession, but the way these processes spill over into daily life is liable to be very different. Affluence and poverty do not co-exist so obviously in Derwentside as in Hackney. Unemployment in Hackney is more likely to run parallel with the occupation of a high rise flat or renting from a private landlord. In Derwentside the loss of employment may find some compensation in the cheap acquisition of a desirable dwelling with a garden.

There are substantial differences between these authorities in terms of claims to buy and completed sales. Hyndburn had a relatively low rate of claims (seven per cent). Hackney, in contrast, with 57 per cent of households in council housing had claims to buy from only two per cent of tenants. Undoubtedly the nature of the dwelling stock

Table 5.2: Case Study Areas: Housing Tenure and Unemployment Rates

	Owner Occupation %	Council Housing %	(Flats as a % of Council Stock) %	Private Renting and Housing Associations %	Unemployment Rate (Males aged 16-59) %	Total Households
Carrick	66.3	20.5	(23.0)	13.2	12.8	28,106
Derwentside	49.3	42.5	(2.7)	8.2	26.0	32,846
Hackney	16.5	57.4	(83.3)	26.0	16.1	68,499
Hounslow	53.1	30.0	(55.7)	16.9	7.4	73,112
Hyndburn	78.0	15.7	(32.6)	6.5	11.8	29,367
New Forest	71.0	15.4	(14.9)	13.8	7.1	53,490

Source: 1981 Census; and Chartered Institute of Public Finance and Accountancy, Housing Rent Statistics, April 1982.

plays a significant part in this. The high proportion of flats in Hackney considerably reduces the propensity to purchase. Derwentside, the area with the highest level of unemployment had the second highest rate of claims (18 per cent). The use of redundancy payments may play some part in this but this is likely to be only a marginal factor. Of greater significance is the combination of relatively attractive dwellings and low valuations. For purchasers in Derwentside it was quite possible to afford to purchase on relatively low incomes or even on state benefits. General house price levels and the relationships between rent levels and mortgage payments may be the most significant factor. Indeed, even if the majority of dwellings in Hackney were attractive to buy, high valuations would exclude many tenants. This factor combines with the large number of flats in Hackney to produce the low rate of claims.

Whilst there are no simple explanations for the variation in levels of sales, authorities like New Forest and Carrick do fit the model of the attractive, rural area with a predominance of council houses (rather than flats), the majority of which are located on smaller estates and in a scattering of villages. The issues in this context revolve around the potential damage to village communities, second homes and the problems of replacement in suitable locations. Hounslow, which like Hackney has a high proportion of flats in the stock, also presents a very different picture in terms of the local labour market. The adjacency of Heathrow airport is a significant factor in sustaining a sub-section of council tenants on relatively high incomes employed at the airport and in related activities. Whilst house prices are high many tenants are in a position to meet those costs, indicating the likelihood of a significant depletion of the stock of houses.

The differences in residential valuations between localities must be a major consideration in assessing the unevenness in the propensity to buy among council tenants. In Hyndburn and Derwentside, for example, almost all properties valued in 1980/81 had valuations of less than £15,000 and the majority were below £10,000. Hounslow, and more particularly Hackney, present a significant contrast. Valuations there began at the highest valuations in Hyndburn and Derwentside; almost half the properties sold in Hackney were valued at above £30,000. This obviously reflects general price trends in the London housing market and has clear implications for the likely number of tenants who can afford to buy in those circumstances. Even with discounts of 50 or 60 per cent, prices can be around £20,000.

But for the tenant who can afford to buy in a high valuation area the potential gains are substantial. For example, a 50 per cent discount in Hackney could be worth around £20,000 in 1981. In the same year a similar level of discount in Hyndburn represented around £7,000. There is no reason to suppose that these differentials have changed since then. Indeed, given the pattern of the recession, it is more likely that the valuation gap has widened between affluent and less affluent areas. The illogicalities of the private market produce a situation where two years' tenancy in one authority can be worth considerably more than 30 or 40 years' tenancy somewhere else.

Thus the relationship between average incomes and average discounted price varies enormously between localities. For example, in Derwentside the ratio of average price to average income is almost one to one, whereas it is about two to one in Hounslow. For those in employment in the more depressed areas, therefore, price barriers are not an issue. But in inner London they clearly are, and this is reflected in the typical purchasing household which tends to have multiple earners. In Hackney 75 per cent of households buying their council house in 1981 had at least three adults in the dwelling.

It is perhaps ironic that Derwentside (and similar areas) have in many ways the most propitious combination of local factors for the large scale sale of council houses. A relatively depressed owner-occupied market producing low valuations, pressure on council rents and a predominance of three bedroomed houses mean that for many tenants the right to buy is both attractive and feasible. In contrast, Hackney, which from tenure characteristics might be presented as the area with the highest frustrated demand for home ownership, has the least favourable circumstances. There, despite rising rents, the costs of renting still lag far behind the equivalent in mortgage payments, while the majority of dwellings are flats. The circumstances in Hackney point to a further ghettoisation of the most disadvantaged. What is presented as the satisfaction of frustrated desires to purchase is severely distorted by the contours of market prices and local economic circumstances. What makes sense and what is feasible for individual households are a product of specific local factors rather than an expression of innate desires.

It would, however, be misleading to suggest that in areas where valuations are low the opportunities and abilities to purchase are evenly distributed. Whilst redundancy payments have played some part in sales in Derwentside, they remain a marginal factor. By and large those who buy are joint earning households in what appears to be relatively stable employment. Whilst in 1981 the unemployment rate for males aged 16-59 was 27 per cent, only 27 per cent of purchaser households had been in their present employment for three years or less. More than a third of principal earners had been in their present jobs for more than ten years, and almost a quarter for more than 15 years.

HOUSING AND MARGINALITY

The relationship between rental and mortgage costs is a crucial feature of the sales policy. As the costs of renting have escalated and moved nearer to market levels, home ownership has benefitted from generous subsidies, tax concessions, and (at times) lower interest rates. The high discounts available under the right to buy are perhaps the most extreme example. But the costs and meanings of purchase are very different between localities and have varied significantly over time. For some, ownership is achieved and sustained at very considerable expense. For others, council house purchase can mean an immediate reduction in outgoings associated with housing. Those who purchased under discretionary policies in the late 1960s and early 1970s conformed, by and large, to the image of the relatively affluent working class household, occupying a more attractive dwelling and (probably) benefiting from the sales policy through choice. Only a small discount of 10-20 per cent was on offer. It is likely that in most cases the immediate costs of owning were higher than rental payments. The situation is now dramatically changed. The Housing and Building Control Act, 1984 offers discounts of up to 60 per cent and to remain as a tenant promises a lower quality service at even higher cost. What may have been an expression of choice in the 1960s may now be an expression of constraint. The purchase of a council dwelling may be a way of escaping from rising costs in the state housing sector and have little to do with preferences for home ownership as such. If present trends continue, it will become increasingly difficult to 'read off' patterns of sales as indicators of relative affluence or the fulfilment of innate desires. In different localities sales will be representative of quite different circumstances. A national policy offering subsidy based on dwelling valuations, which vary greatly, produces peculiar results. Indeed, it is ironic that the potential for privatisation may be highest in those areas where the residential built environment has the lowest valuation. It is in these areas that on present policies rental costs are more likely to exceed purchase costs. The nature of the council dwelling stock will play a significant role in what happens in these circumstances.

It is undoubtedly the case that we are seeing a significant restructuring of housing tenure in this country. The contraction of council housing is indicative of a major shift in emphasis in working class housing provision and in the nature of the welfare state. This is taking place against a backcloth of economic recession, the weakening of organised labour, and the reassertion of market forces guided and facilitated through a strong, centralised state. It was argued earlier that part of the explanation for what is happening to council housing derives from the

Table 5.3: Factors Influencing the Likely Coincidence of Council Housing with Marginality

	Size of Rented Sector (Public & private)	Differentiation within Council Stock	Residential Values	Size of Buying/ Renting Cost Gap	Impact of Recession	Likely Coincidence of Council Housing with Marginality
A	High	High	High	High	High	High
B	Low	Low	Low	Low	High	High
C	Low	Low	High	High	Low	High
D	High	High	Low	Low	High	Moderate

expansion of a surplus population, disadvantaged and marginalised as both producers and consumers. But the coincidence of this marginalised population with council housing is not uniform, nor will it necessarily become more marked. Disinvestment in new production and disposals through sales are the key housing policies influencing this relationship in the present phase, but the historical development of council housing is highly varied as are local labour and housing markets. The impact of economic restructuring and economic decline is uneven, and the meanings and attributes of different forms of housing provision vary in significant ways. The social reputation and status of council housing differs. It is neither uniformly superior nor inferior to home ownership. In some areas the high quality house with a garden is representative of the council housing sector and is an aspiration for many owner occupiers of dwellings which lack these attributes. Preferences for home ownership vary across the country and it is not the case that where levels of owner occupation are lowest the aspirations are highest. Relative tenure costs and aspects of quality combine with less tangible factors, such as differential class imagery and what is regarded as normal and natural, to produce different patterns. It is clear, therefore, that the coincidence of marginality with council housing will be varied. It is also true that patterns of privatisation through sales will vary over space and time; there is no fixed pool of demand. Material considerations related to movements in mortgage interest rates, rent levels and changes in government policy aimed at encouraging a greater shift from collective to individualised forms of provision will influence the future progress of sales. Residential values reflecting the economic circumstances of localities will also be a crucial factor.

Table 5.3 lists some of the key factors which will influence the pattern of sales, and the strength of the link between council tenancy and marginalisation. Other factors could be added and the table is not intended as an exhaustive representation of the possible relationships. Moreover, it concentrates on the more evident variations in relative costs, economic decline and current patterns of housing provision. It would be wrong to underestimate local variations in class structure and class consciousness which may have contributed to quite striking variations in the propensity to buy council dwellings in different localities.

A describes a locality with a large public stock highly differentiated in terms of dwelling type and quality, where poverty co-exists with high valuations in the local housing market. Movement out of council housing through sales will be limited and selective. An increasing coincidence of unemployment, low pay and other forms of marginalisation with council housing would be the expectation.

B is also representative of a locality suffering high employment and low wages but has a small stock of high quality, low priced council houses. In some cases, ownership may be the cheaper option. It may also be the case that less selective movement out of council housing is combined with high unemployment among existing owner occupiers. In other words, it may be more adequately described as a marginalised locality.

C describes an area where the local economy is relatively healthy, where the council stock is predominantly houses with gardens and where the cost gap is high. There is a very small privately rented sector and the marginalised minority are concentrated in council housing. The cost gap is liable to produce selective movement out but, compared with A, it will not produce such a coincidence of low quality or unpopular housing with other aspects of disadvantage.

D is typical of a depressed metropolitan area where private renting remains high in the inner areas. The council stock is highly differentiated and residential values are relatively low. Whilst movement out through sales is likely to be highly selective, the surplus or marginal population will be concentrated in renting generally, rather than council housing in particular. In such a locality the impact of rising rents combined with higher discounts and lower mortgage cost is less predictable. Will an increasing number of tenants be encouraged to purchase high rise flats or less popular houses as a response to rising rental costs? In those circumstances, purchase for many households would represent a strategy for coping with reduced rental subsidies. The accumulative potential and resale value of some dwellings would be minimal but day-to-day cost of ownership may be lower than renting.

The connection, therefore, between the marginal population and housing provision take on different forms in different locations. In some areas the dominant form of working class housing provision has been either private renting or owner occupation. In some situations marginal groups will be identified with areas of owner-occupied run-down older terraced dwellings or inner area private renting. The emergent surplus population may be most concentrated in areas of lower quality council housing in the urban centres or on stigmatised peripheral estates, but the reassertion of the connections between local incomes and housing disadvantage is not limited to that tenure.

CONCLUDING COMMENTS

This chapter has tried to set the issue of council house sales and disinvestment from council housing in the context of a more general restructuring of welfare provision. Collective housing is being progressively marginalised and the dominant mode of state subsidised individualised provision is becoming more segmented and stratified. The rapid growth of unemployment and the consequent weakening of organised labour have facilitated a renegotiation of the class compromise around the welfare state. The pattern of privatisation in housing is uneven and linked to an unevenness in economic restructuring and economic decline. From a consideration of the national and regional trends in council house sales there is an apparent North-South dimension and a contrast between inner and outer urban areas. But the case study material suggests that we need to look behind tenure labels to appreciate the meaning and significance of sales. Similar rates of sales in different localities need not necessarily reflect similar circumstances. The position of marginal groups in the housing market revolves, therefore, not only around the erosion of council housing but relates to the circumstances in which households enter home ownership. At a general level, and this will vary by locality and over time, the process of marginalisation will increasingly spill over and erode the perceived connections between home ownership and social status. The more drastic the inducements for tenants to purchase and the more complete the transfer of council housing into owner occupation, the more stratified and differentiated the latter tenure will become.

But for those experiencing unemployment, low pay and insecure earnings, and for a mass of working class elderly, fully excluded from the labour market with little reward, home ownership under any terms may offer more risks than compensations. Stated bluntly, it is not tenure divisions but class divisions which remain paramount.

This chapter is based on research which was funded by the Nuffield Foundation.

Chapter Six

THE EFFECT OF SALES ON THE PUBLIC SECTOR IN SCOTLAND

Michael Foulis

INTRODUCTION

        One of the key elements recently producing change
in the public sector has been the government's policy on
sales to sitting tenants, especially the right to buy.   The
policy has been the subject of some discussion, but most of
it so far has concerned the influence of sales on the public
sector in England and Wales.   This chapter will attempt to
redress the balance slightly by examining several measures of
the effect of sales on the very different public sector in
Scotland, drawing on work undertaken in the Scottish
Development Department (SDD).   The picture these measures
reveal will help us in assessing the extent to which sales
policy really has had, or is likely to have, a major impact
on the quality, size and distribution of the largest Scottish
tenure.

The Scottish Public Sector
        The Scottish public sector is commonly regarded as
large and dominating.   Internationally, it is relatively
bigger than that of certain eastern European countries.   In
1981 it contained around one million dwellings, or over half
the total Scottish stock of some two million.   As well as
council and new town housing, the public sector in Scotland
includes the stock of the Scottish Special Housing
Association (SSHA).   In some major centres of population,
such as the block formed by the districts of Falkirk, West
Lothian, Cumbernauld and Kilsyth, Motherwell and Monklands,
the public sector reduced owner occupation and private
renting to less than 30 per cent of the stock.   Yet, in
other parts of Scotland public provision was as low as in the
most heavily owner-occupied regions of England and Wales:
in Eastwood it had only 11 per cent of the stock, in Bearsden
and Milngavie 15 per cent, in Skye and Lochalsh 16 per cent,
and in Orkney and the Western Isles 21 per cent.

86

The physical form that public provision took was not uniform either. The 1981 Census revealed that half the public sector tenants in Scotland occupied detached, semi-detached or terraced houses. In the four cities of Aberdeen, Dundee, Edinburgh and Glasgow, however, this proportion fell to under one quarter, while in many rural districts it rose to over four-fifths.

The role of the public sector in housing different social and occupational groups has also varied from area to area. As we see in Table 6.1, households with an unskilled or a semi-skilled manual head were generally more likely to be in public renting than households with skilled manual or white collar heads. However, if we compare the level of public renting in a particular occupational group with the average level for all groups in an area, there are significant differences. These are shown in the 'relative likelihood' statistics given in the table.

Taking two extremes: unskilled manual heads were 7.63 times more likely than average to be public tenants in Eastwood, but only 1.14 times more likely than average in Motherwell; and semi-skilled manual heads were 4.24 and 1.11 times more likely than the average to be so in the same two districts. The effect of this variation was that Scotland contained both areas where public renting was more the particular tenure of low earning groups, and areas where it was less the particular tenure of these groups, than England and Wales as a whole. From these three measures we can see that the Scottish public sector, though large overall, varied considerably from area to area. Thus, we might expect the effect of sales on that public sector also to vary.

GOVERNMENT POLICY ON SALES SINCE 1970

Before examining what the effect of the current government's sales policy has been, it is helpful to provide an historical perspective by looking at how that policy developed during previous administrations. Indeed, since the early 1970s, sales policy has undergone a number of substantial shifts. These have been reflected in a broadly similar way on both sides of the border, despite the differences noted above.

Sales Policy 1972-1979
Sales of council houses have never been entirely ruled out by central government, though up to March 1972 the specific consent of the Secretary of State for Scotland was required in each case. At that date, the then Conservative government removed this requirement and introduced a general consent. Discounts of up to 20 per cent were available depending on the purchaser's length of tenancy.

Table 6.1: Proportion of Different Occupational Groups in Public Renting, and 'Relative Likelihood' of being in Public Renting, 1981

Households headed by	EASTWOOD		MOTHERWELL		SCOTLAND		ENGLAND & WALES	
	%	'Relative Likelihood'	%	'Relative Likelihood'	%	'Relative Likelihood'	%	'Relative Likelihood'
Professional	1.5	0.15	21.2	0.26	8.9	0.16	3.5	0.12
Employers and Managers	2.5	0.25	46.6	0.58	21.1	0.39	7.5	0.26
Intermediate Non-Manual	4.3	0.42	56.9	0.70	28.3	0.52	10.6	0.37
Junior Non-Manual	5.6	0.55	75.5	0.94	43.3	0.79	18.4	0.64
Skilled Manual and Own Account Non-Professional	19.8	1.94	84.6	1.05	64.3	1.18	31.3	1.09
Semi-Skilled Manual and Personal Service	43.3	4.24	89.8	1.11	69.0	1.26	42.1	1.46
Unskilled Manual	77.8	7.63	92.1	1.14	81.0	1.48	56.0	1.94

Table 6.1 (Contd.)

Households headed by	EASTWOOD %	'Relative Likelihood'	MOTHERWELL %	'Relative Likelihood'	SCOTLAND %	'Relative Likelihood'	ENGLAND & WALES %	'Relative Likelihood'
Total (including Never Active and Inadequately Defined)	10.2	1.00	80.8	1.00	54.6	1.00	28.8	1.00

Note: 'Relative Likelihood' is calculated by dividing the percentage of each group in public renting by the percentage of all groups in public renting. For example, households headed by professionals in Motherwell were 0.26 times as likely to be in the public sector as were all households there.

Source: OPCS, 1981 Census, 10% Small Area Statistics (Table 49); and GB Report (Table 47).

89

In 1974 the incoming Labour government reversed the Scottish situation and reinstated the requirement for the Secretary of State's consent to each sale; in England and Wales the general consent introduced in 1970 continued. An SDD circular indicated that consent would be granted only where authorities could demonstrate that there was no significant unsatisfied demand for houses to rent in their areas. The circular also made a five year pre-emption clause obligatory, and withdrew the discount. The effect of these policy shifts is shown in Table 6.2.

Table 6.2: Public Sector Sales in Scotland, 1971, 1973 and 1975

	1971		1973		1975	
	No.	%	No.	%	No.	%
LA	99	(38)	708	(35)	24	(9)
SSHA	1	(..)	204	(10)	6	(2)
New Town	159	(61)	1,136	(55)	247	(89)
TOTAL	259	(100)	2,048	(100)	277	(100)

Source: Watson (1977).

The effect on overall public sector sales was dramatic, but the provisions of the 1974 circular seem to have had a particularly marked effect on local authority (compared with SSHA and new town) sales, which dropped from 708 in 1971 to 24 in 1975.

Sales Policy 1979-1980

Policy continued unchanged until the 1979 general election. In May 1979, very soon after the new Conservative administration took office, another circular was issued which reinstated the general consent to sell to sitting tenants, but excluded sheltered and special housing. Discounts also reappeared and were raised to range from 30 per cent to 50 per cent. The obligatory five year pre-emption period, however, remained. The circular stated that the Secretary of State intended to introduce legislation giving sitting tenants a right to buy. Local authorities were urged to put this into effect before the legislation was enacted. Table 6.3 shows the effect on sales of this circular; the figures are not quite comparable to those in Table 6.2 but the great increase, particularly in local authority and SSHA sales, is clear.

Public Sector Sales in Scotland

Table 6.3:   Public Sales in Scotland, 1978 and 1979/80

| | 1978 | | 1979/80* | |
	No.	%	No.	%
LA	105	(14)	2,296	(41)
SSHA	4	(1)	2,388	(42)
New Town	636	(85)	949	(17)
TOTAL	745	(100)	5,633	(100)

* 1979 (Q4) to 1980 (Q3)

Source: SDD, Scottish Housing Statistics, No. 14, HMSO,
          1981;   and SDD, S.3 Returns.

Sales Policy after October 1980 and the Right to Buy
          The right-to-buy provisions of the Tenants' Rights,
Etc. (Scotland) Act, 1980 were brought into effect in October
of that year.   The right to buy was extended to all houses
except sheltered houses, and to all tenants who had been
resident in a public sector house for three years. Discounts
started at 33 per cent and increased by one per cent for
every year of tenancy to a maximum of 50 per cent. The
obligatory pre-emption clause was lifted, and pre-emption was
ruled out except for housing specially adapted for the
elderly or disabled (and also for rural housing in areas
where over one-third of the public stock had been sold and
the Secretary of State was satisfied that an unreasonable
proportion was being resold as holiday homes).   However, a
clawback arrangement whereby if a house was resold within one
year of purchase all the discount would have to be repaid,
within two years, 80 per cent, and so on up until after the
fifth year.   The act also conferred on purchasers the right
to a local authority mortgage calculated on the basis of
their income and age, provided they had evidence of failure
to obtain a sufficient loan from a building society.
          The arrangements for amenity housing for the
elderly were almost immediately changed by the Tenants'
Rights, Etc. (Scotland) Amendment Act, 1980 which became law
in November.   (This legislation followed an agreement
between the government and opposition to avoid delay to the
passage of the (English and Welsh) Housing Bill after Lords'
amendments had been passed shortly before the summer recess;
see Murie (1982) for details.)   In addition to the
discretion to apply a pre-emption clause, local authorities
were now given the opportunity to apply to the Secretary of

State to refuse right-to-buy applications for this type of
housing where they thought it in the community's interest to
do so.

Since 1980 the government has made a number of
other adjustments to their sales policy. In 1983 the
maximum discount was increased from 50 per cent to 60 per
cent (though the increased discount was initially at local
authorities' discretion), benefiting tenants of over 20
years' standing. The government also introduced the
Tenants' Rights, Etc. (Scotland) Amendment Act, 1983 which,
inter alia, made several alterations to the right to buy
itself. These were in brief: a statutory increase in
maximum discount from 50 per cent to 60 per cent; a
reduction in the minimum qualifying period from three to two
years (and a reduction in the minimum discount to 32 per
cent); removal of landlords' discretion not to count time
spent in the house as a child for discount; removal of the
12 month ban on re-application after withdrawal; changes to
the arrangements for teachers' houses in islands authorities;
and an extension of the types of public sector tenancies
counting towards the discount.

Differences between Scotland and England and Wales
One of the main differences is that in England and
Wales local authorities may seek the appropriate Secretary of
State's permission to impose a ten year pre-emption on all
sales in designated rural areas. The right to buy also
includes tenants of non-charitable English and Welsh housing
associations (though in 1985 the government announced that it
would legislate to extend this provision to Scotland). The
Secretary of State for Scotland may decide to hold a public
local inquiry to determine whether a local authority has
failed to carry out its statutory duty; so far this has
happened three times, involving Dundee, Stirling and East
Lothian district councils. However, south of the border the
Secretary of State for the Environment (or Wales) may
intervene if he feels that local authorities are not
prosecuting their obligations with sufficient vigour, and
direct his officials to make sales and grant mortgages
themselves; this has occurred once, in Norwich.

MEASURES OF THE EFFECT OF PUBLIC SECTOR SALES

Measuring the Extent of Sales
Volume: Nearly 44,000 public sector houses were sold to
their occupants in the four and a half years between April
1979 and September 1983 (these figures may understate the
true position because some districts have been slow to make
returns, especially for 1983). Local authority sales
accounted for 28,700 of these, SSHA sales for 7,500 and new
town sales for 7,500. This represents a much higher
proportion of the new town stock (13.2 per cent) and of the

SSHA stock (8 per cent) than of the local authority stock (3.2 per cent). Thus, new town and SSHA tenants have appeared, so far, much more willing, or able, to buy than local authority tenants.

Timing: As we can see in Figure 6.1, the rate of sales increased fairly steadily from the beginning of 1981. The SSHA and new town rates fluctuated around the same level from about the end of 1980 (300-600 per quarter), so the overall increase was mainly contributed by the local authorities. Their rate of sales rose steadily from the introduction of the right to buy until about the first quarter of 1983, when it exceeded 3,000 per quarter. It then fell back in quarters two and three, though most of the drop was probably due to late returns. Once a rough adjustment has been made for the missing local authorities, the underlying rate appears to be about 2,900 sales per quarter, or roughly one and a quarter per cent of the local authority stock per annum. The rates in the SSHA and new towns were again roughly two per cent and two and three quarter per cent respectively per annum, giving an overall total of around 15,000 public sector sales per annum. The right to buy appears to have narrowed the gap between, on the one hand, the local authority, and, on the other, the new town and SSHA rates of sales, but it has not been closed.

Location: As we might have expected, Figure 6.2 shows that the level of sales varied between local authority districts. Tenants have been exercising their right to buy most extensively in the smaller or rural districts: Stewartry, North East Fife and the Western Isles all sold over ten per cent of the stock they had in April 1979, and Badenoch and Strathspey, Eastwood, Orkney, Perth and Kinross, and Kincardine and Deeside over nine per cent. The right to buy was, on the other hand, least exercised by tenants of the urban authorities in the central belt: Dundee, Dumbarton and Monklands (and also the mainly rural Clydesdale) sold under one per cent, and Clydebank, Motherwell, Glasgow, Cumnock and Doon Valley, Hamilton, Stirling, and Kilmarnock and Loudon under two per cent. Broadly, this pattern corresponded with variations in the level of public renting. Sales were most extensive where the public sector share was already smallest. Sales have probably increased, rather than decreased, the variety that we noted above in the Scottish public sector.

Type: Most of the properties sold have been detached, semi-detached, and terraced houses, which are commonly regarded, other things being equal, as the 'best' stock. These types have accounted for, on average, 87 per cent of local authority, 88 per cent of new town, and 97 per cent of

Figure 6.1: Sales to Sitting Tenants in Scotland, 1979 to 1983

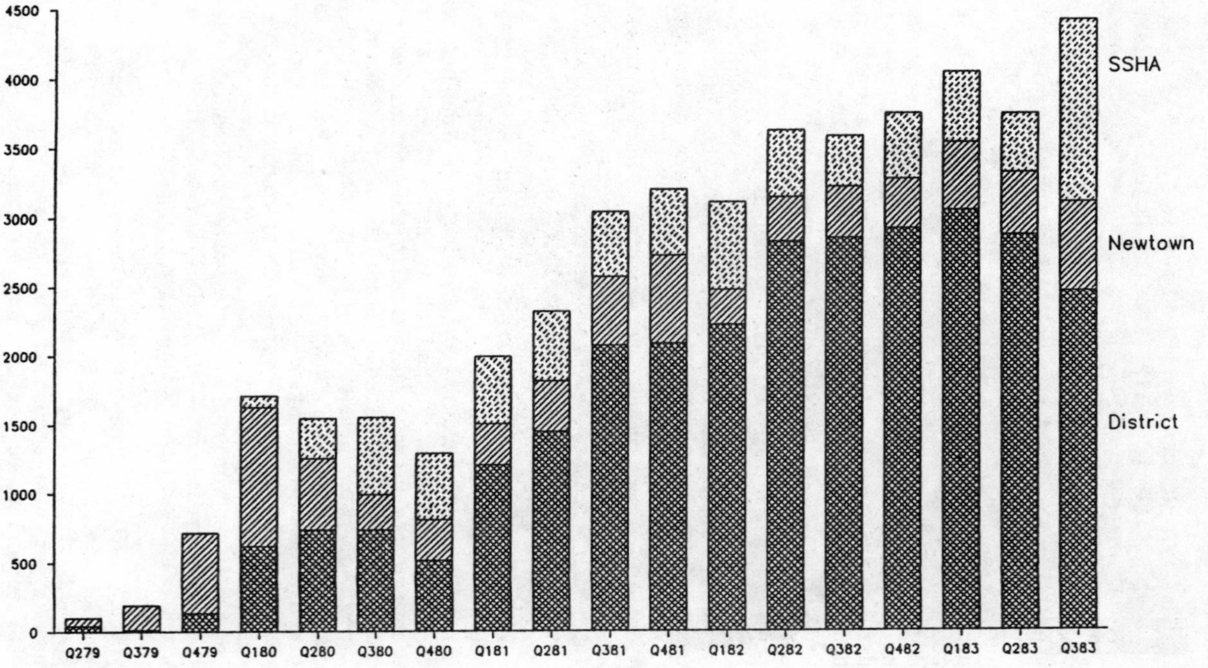

94

Figure 6.2: Sales to Sitting Tenants in Scotland, Q1 1979 to Q3 1983, as Percentage of District Stock at April 1979

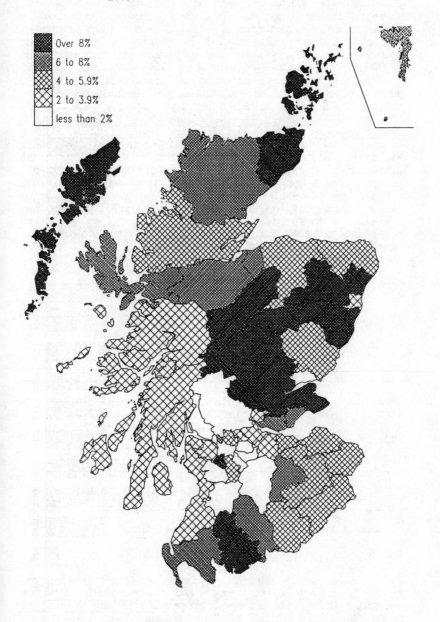

SSHA sales. Unfortunately, we do not have very precise information on the size of the local authority, new town and SSHA stock of detached, semi-detached and terraced houses. However, it is possible to make a rough calculation by combining the figures from the 1981 Census with departmental estimates for the same period and making a one per cent allowance for vacancy where appropriate. On this basis the 39,000 sales of houses between April 1979 and September 1983 represented about six per cent of the local authorities', about twelve per cent of the SSHA's, and about 16 per cent of the new towns' stock of this type of property.

Tenure Balance: Given the fairly low level of sales we have been considering above, it is not surprising that they have had little directly discernible effect so far on the broad brush published estimates of the tenure split in Scotland. However, there can be no doubt that they were having some effect: as Table 6.4 shows, since 1981 sales have exceeded the level of private sector completions, more than doubling the rate of increase in owner occupation. Since 1981 they have also exceeded the level of public sector completions, thus, other things being equal, decreasing the size and not just the share of that sector.

Table 6.4: Sales and Completions in Scotland, 1979-83

| | | Completions* | |
	Public Sales	Public Sector	Private Sector
1979	1,419	8,063	15,175
1980	6,484	7,488	12,242
1981	11,019	7,066	11,021
1982	15,058	3,733	11,514
1983	18,315	3,492	13,178
TOTAL	52,295	29,842	63,130

* Both columns exclude housing associations.

Source: SDD, Statistical Bulletin, HSIU No. 16.

We can examine the effects of these trends over time by using a fairly rough and ready model which was described in the SDD study of Movement into and within the Owner Occupied Sector of the Housing Market (McQueen, 1983). This model takes the tenure balance revealed by the

1981 Census and projects on it the effects of different rates of completions, sales and demolitions over a ten year period. Table 6.5 shows the results produced by a variety of assumptions about these rates. Average rates of completions between quarter 1 of 1980 and quarter 2 of 1983, and the recent rate of sales (one and a half per cent per annum) decreased the public sector share from 55 per cent to 45 per cent, and increased the owner occupier share from 35 per cent to 45 per cent over the ten year period. Interestingly, the relative shares of the different tenures were not greatly affected by what might be regarded as reasonable variations in completion rates. They were, however, more sensitive to variations in the rate of sales, since sales have the double action of simultaneously increasing the private sector and decreasing the public sector.

We can see this quite clearly in some of the other combinations shown in Table 6.5. With no sales, recent (quarter 1 of 1980 to quarter 3 of 1983) average trends in completion would produce a tenure split of 53 per cent public rented, 38 per cent owner occupied and nine per cent private rented and other by 1991. The overall size of the public sector would still exceed one million. However, if we added the recent average rate of sales (one and a half per cent per annum), then the quite substantial shift of the tenure balance noted above would be produced: to 45 per cent public rented, 45 per cent owner occupied and nine per cent private rented and other; and on these assumptions the public sector would drop to just over 870,000 dwellings. Variations in the rate of completions, within reasonable bounds, had little effect. Decreasing public sector completions to 3,000 per annum and raising owner occupation ones to 15,000 per annum only shifts the balance to 44 per cent public rented, 47 per cent owner occupied and nine per cent private renting and other.

Thus, we can be fairly confident that, in the medium term, the public sector will remain as a major feature of the Scottish housing scene; even if the current, historically high, level of sales was to continue, it would be unlikely to drop below, say, 850,000 dwellings or 44 per cent of the stock in 1991.

In the longer term, what would be required to reduce the Scottish public sector to the share held by the English and Welsh one in 1981 (29 per cent)? To reach that level by 2001 (that is over 20 years from the 1981 position), on completion trends (from Q1 of 1982 to Q2 of 1983), sales would have almost to double, to two and three quarter per cent per annum. Even to extend owner occupation in Scotland to over 50 per cent of households by the turn of the century would require sales to sustain themselves at around one per cent per annum.

Table 6.5: Tenure Balance in 1991 based on varying
assumptions of Completions and Sales projected
from 1981 Census

Sales	Completions		Tenure Balance		
	Public Rented[1]	Owner Occupied[2]	Public Rented	Owner Occupied	Private Rented & Other (inc. HAs)
			%	%	
0.0%	Low	High	51	40	9
	Average	Average	53	38	9
	High	Low	54	37	9
0.5%	Low	High	49	42	9
	Average	Average	50	40	9
	High	Low	52	39	9
1.0%	Low	High	46	44	9
	Average	Average	48	43	9
	High	Low	49	41	9
1.5%	Low	High	44	47	9
	Average	Average	45	45	9
	High	Low	47	44	9
Tenure Balance in 1981			55	35	11

Notes: For a description of the model which produced these
figures see SDD (1983), p.74.

1: Low = 3,000 pa;   average = 5,658 pa;
high = 9,000 pa.

2: High = 15,000 pa;   average = 11,725 pa;
low = 9,000 pa.

In each case the average figure is actual rate of
completions, Q1 1980 to Q2 1983.

Conclusion: We have examined several measures concerned
with the extent of the effects of sales on the public sector
in Scotland.   These indicated that, under current
conditions, sales were helping to move towards a smaller
public sector, which had fewer houses and which was more

concentrated in the urban areas where it was largest already. Indeed, it is clear that, unless completions and demolitions increase really dramatically, sales are in general the biggest single influence on public sector change, affecting its size, composition and distribution. However, after four and a half years of general consent and three years of the right to buy the rate of movement had been gradual rather than spectacular. No district had sold over one eighth of its stock, there was no discernible effect recorded on the tenure balance, and the public sector was unlikely to approach the 1981 English and Welsh share even by the turn of the century (by which time, of course, the latter is likely, on present trends, to have been significantly reduced).

Measures of the Spatial Concentration of Sales

This overall low level of sales could, however, still be of considerable local significance were it focused into powerful spatial concentrations. We have already looked at the concentration of sales at local authority district level; we now proceed to a finer level of disaggregation, and, with the help of the 1981 Census small area statistics, examine concentrations in enumeration districts (EDs).

These EDs are small areas containing around 100 households on average. Public sector households were found in roughly 12,600 of the 18,000 Scottish EDs (after adjusting for sales between April 1979 and the census in April 1981). EDs usually contain households of different tenures, but the public sector tended to be fairly concentrated (for example, half the EDs with public sector households had less than 25 per cent of other tenures and two-fifths had less than 10 per cent).

The census figures, of course, only give us numbers of households present and not the stock of different tenures; any percentage sales figures we calculate will be more or less accurate depending on the local number of sharing households or vacant properties. The effect of sharing households is probably insignificant, since the census recorded very few of these in Scotland, and they tended not to be particularly associated with the public sector. The number of vacant properties was, however, around 50,000, or five per cent of the public sector, and locally this could impart a significant upward bias to figures of percentage sales. However, since only households with occupants could be sold to their sitting tenant, it may be that the numbers of 'other vacants', 'under construction', etc. were not too important. Unfortunately, the figures also exclude houses which were usually occupied, but which happened to have no one present on census night; around 20,000 were in the public sector. On average this will tend to push up percentage sales figures very slightly; for example, a figure of ten per cent sales will probably be nearer 9.8 per cent in reality. Finally, it is possible to separate out new town EDs, but we cannot distinguish between local authority and SSHA ones. This is unfortunate because of the gap between the rate of local authority and SSHA sales mentioned above.

The two measures of the spatial concentration of sales we shall examine are the proportion of EDs which have experienced sales, and the relative volumes of sales produced by EDs selling high and low proportions of their stock. Were sales highly concentrated, we would expect them to have spread into only a few EDs, and we would also expect the great bulk of them to be found in EDs which had sold all, or nearly all, their public sector stock.

Local Authority/SSHA and New Towns: Both measures, however, revealed a fairly even spread of sales across local authority/SSHA and new town areas.   Overall, between April 1979 and June 1983, sales to sitting tenants penetrated into just over half of the EDs with local authority or SSHA households.   In the new towns, with their higher level of sales, around seven-eighths of the public sector had experienced sales.   Under one and a half per cent (or 428) of LA/SSHA and half a per cent (or 35) of new town sales were produced by EDs which had sold over half their stock. Three-quarters of LA/SSHA sales came from EDs which had sold 15 per cent or less.   The new towns' higher overall level of sales seemed to derive, in part, from EDs where 21-50 per cent had been sold.

Semi-detached or Terraced Houses and Low Rise Flats: LA/SSHA: Since these made up the bulk of sales, the position was broadly similar for house sales as it was for total sales.   Both measures revealed a wide spread: 63 per cent of EDs containing semi-detached or terraced houses had experienced sales;   only two and a half per cent of these sales came from EDs which had sold over half of their stock, whereas three-fifths came from those selling 15 per cent or less.   Again, one of the reasons why house sales were relatively higher than total sales was that there was a greater concentration of the former in EDs where between eleven per cent and 25 per cent of the houses had been bought.   Sales of low rise flats, however, appear to have been slightly more concentrated: only 21 per cent of EDs with them had sold any;   nearly one-fifth of the sales came from EDs which had sold over half, and 12.5 per cent from areas selling out completely.

Semi-detached and Terraced Houses and Low Rise Flats: New Towns: The pattern in the new towns was rather different; here house, and especially flat, sales were more extensive: 88 per cent and 57 per cent respectively of the relevant EDs had experienced sales.   The distribution of low rise flat sales was also closer to that of house sales. For instance, only two per cent of the low rise flat sales were found in the EDs where over half the tenants had bought. The relatively high level of sales of new town houses and flats was mainly produced by the areas where a fifth to a half of the relevant stock had been bought.

Low Rise Flats: Edinburgh: It is interesting to compare low rise flat sales in Edinburgh with those in LA/SSHA areas generally. Edinburgh is the only local authority to have sold this type of property in any significant numbers: in the last quarter of 1982 they made up 40 per cent of the city's total sales, against 17 per cent in Glasgow. The importance of low rise flats in the two cities was, however, very similar: 45 per cent of the public sector (including SSHA) in Edinburgh and 48 per cent in Glasgow. If anything, sales in Edinburgh were more concentrated despite their higher level. Nearly half (49 per cent) of EDs with low rise flats had sold some, but almost 24 per cent of the sales came from areas which had disposed of over half their supply. This evidence seems to suggest that low rise flat buyers were more particular about where they bought, or were maybe more in need of the support of other buyers near at hand. But even in Edinburgh, sales of this type were still fairly well spread around: over half were in areas where 15 per cent or less of the stock had been sold.

Urban and Rural Areas: The census also allows us to look at the concentration of sales in settlements of different sizes: from the continuously built up area of the Clydeside conurbation, with a population of over one million in 1981, to isolated dwellings and villages with populations of under 1,000. As Table 6.6 indicates, the more rural the area, the higher the proportion of its stock which had been sold, and also the more widespread were the sales (this corresponds with the pattern illustrated in Figure 6.2 above).

The most rural areas (settlements of 1,000 or less), however, managed to combine the highest level of sales overall (6.22 per cent) with a relatively low level of penetration: only 47 per cent of EDs had sales. This position was achieved by concentration. The effect was not limited to a few rural areas; only in North-East Fife, Caithness and Inverness did the proportion of EDs with sales exceed 60 per cent. In the rural parts of Ettrick and Lauderdale, Moray, Nairn, Clydesdale, Angus, and Orkney and Shetland it dropped below the 36 per cent found in the Clydeside conurbation.

Table 6.6: Sales to Sitting Tenants in Urban and Rural
Scotland (excluding New Towns)

Size of Settlement (Pop. 1981)	Stock Sold	EDs with Sales
	%	%
Over 1,000,000 (Clydeside Conurbation)	1.84	36.25
1,000,000 - 100,000	2.76	48.68
100,000 - 10,000	4.51	68.14
10,000 - 1,000	4.88	68.20
1,000 or less	6.22	48.60
Scotland	3.47	52.85

Note: Sales from Q2 of 1979 to Q2 of 1983 in non-New Town
EDs. Stock from 1981 Census plus pre-census sales.

These figures appear to indicate quite large
contrasts between parts of the countryside where sales were
more popular with tenants than they were elsewhere, and parts
where they were as unpopular as in the major cities. However,
the concentration was not particularly marked; only six per
cent of the sales from this type of area were found in EDs
which had sold over half their stock, and over three-fifths
were in EDs which had sold 15 per cent or less.

The overall distribution of these rural sales was
quite different from that of the Clydeside conurbation, which
had a lower level and more even spread. Eighty six per
cent of the sales came from EDs where 15 per cent or lower of
the tenants bought, only one per cent from EDs where over 50
per cent had bought, and only one per cent from EDs where
between one quarter and one half had bought (though this
latter figure was 13 per cent in the rural areas).

These two measures indicate that, far from being
spatially concentrated, sales tended to be thinly and evenly
distributed round the parts of the public sector they had
spread into. This applied equally to areas where sales had
been low, the Clydeside conurbation, and to areas where they
had been relatively high including the new towns.

Concentration: Sales and the 'Best' Areas
It has been long recognised that there is
considerable variation in the quality of different parts of
the public sector. This arises not just from building type,
but also from the general status of the area in which the
dwellings are found. So it was also generally expected that

the stock sold would not only be of the 'best' types (houses with gardens), but would also be in the 'best' areas, leading in time to a deterioration in the quality of the accommodation which the tenure could offer to people who wished to enter or stay within it.

Unfortunately, it is difficult to define and measure objectively the 'goodness' of different parts of the public sector across the country. One approach would be to apply the SDD Multiple Deprivation Score, which is based on the 1981 Census. This score is primarily a measure of household deprivation, combining into one index the level of overcrowding, young children living above the ground, general and youth unemployment, invalids, one parent and large families, and low earning social economic groups in a particular area. (An area picked out by the score as being badly deprived would be one with high levels of these indicators, and one picked out as having low deprivation would have few vacancies or little unemployment, and few invalids, one parent or large families, young children living above the ground or low earners.) Being a measure of household deprivation, it does not tell us much about the dwellings that tenants have, or have not, been buying. Any deprivation score, high or low, applies to the whole area, and may not fit particularly well with the public sector households in that area (though considerations of the state of the immediate surroundings are obviously important to potential purchasers). The index was also designed for measuring deprivation and not wealth, and so will probably perform better at the bottom end of the scale than at the top. However, with these reservations, it is one of the best comprehensive measures of the state of an area that we have; it is fairly widely known and used in the identification of problem areas and the subsequent targetting of resources.

How is this deprivation index related to the level of sales in different areas? Our first measure of the concentration of sales in the 'best' areas is the correlation between the deprivation score and percentage sales at the ED level. This disaggregated level is probably the best one to work at, since deprivation tends to vary considerably, even within an estate. As we would expect, the more deprived the ED, the lower the percentage of the stock sold was likely to be. However, it was not a very strong relationship, explaining only about six per cent of the variation in LA/SSHA EDs. This was partly due to the large number of EDs with no sales (6,000) but, even after these were excluded, deprivation only explained about twelve per cent of the variation in percentage sales. The relationship was slightly stronger in the new towns where sales were more extensive, but not dramatically so, explaining about eleven per cent of the variation overall, and 16 per cent in the sales EDs only.

103

One problem with these percentage sales figures is that they were rather unreliable at the upper end, since nearly all of the very high percentages stemmed more from a tiny public stock than from a great concentration of sales (for example, the average number of sales in the 186 LA/SSHA EDs which sold out was one and a half). We avoided this problem above by looking at the volume of sales produced by EDs which had sold high or low proportions of their stock. We can also avoid it in our second measure, which looks at the rate of sales in the 'best' one, five and ten per cent, etc. of the stock, or, more strictly, of occupied public sector properties. This is achieved by ranking EDs in order of their deprivation score, and grouping them until as near as possible the 'best' one per cent, etc. of the stock has been built up. Then we can count up the sales in these parts of the stock, and in this way estimate the proportion of, say, the 'best' one per cent of Glasgow's stock that has been sold, or the rate of sales in the part of Glasgow's stock falling into the 'best' one per cent of the Scottish stock.

LA/SSHA and New Towns: Starting at the Scottish level, the proportion of LA/SSHA stock sold was indeed highest in the 'best' parts and tailed off towards the 'worst' parts. However, not even in the best one per cent was over one-eleventh of the stock sold between April 1979 and June 1983; and there were over 200 sales in the 'worst' ten per cent (mainly in Glasgow, Inverclyde, Edinburgh and Cunninghame), and 6,400 in the 'worst' half.
Looking at the new towns again the highest level of sales was not in the 'best' five per cent, but in the next portion, the 'best' five to ten per cent, where 18 per cent of the stock had been sold. Sales were also more evenly distributed across the whole range of the stock: the highest percentage was only 1.6 times the average, whereas it was 2.6 times the average in the LA/SSHA stock. This only partially reflected the relative lack of deprivation in the new towns, since if we divide the new towns' stock up into the LA/SSHA bands, then the distribution of sales was still much more even, and the rates higher in every category, than in the LA/SSHA stock.

Glasgow and Edinburgh: These two cities have historically had rather different approaches to sales. Edinburgh was active in the early 1970s, and began to sell again by the beginning of 1980. Glasgow, however, waited for the right to buy, and sales did not come through in any numbers until the beginning of 1982. Their public sectors differed too: Glasgow's had a much larger share of the city's total stock than had Edinburgh's, 63 per cent compared to 32 per cent (in 1981); and deprivation was deeper and more extensive in Glasgow: 26 per cent of Glasgow's, but only 13 per cent of Edinburgh's, stock fell into the Scottish LA/SSHA 'worst' ten

per cent, and four per cent and one per cent respectively
into the 'worst' one per cent.

Indeed, sales were higher and more extensive in
Edinburgh: the highest rate was in the 'best' one to five
per cent category where 17 per cent of the stock was sold.
The pattern was similar, though lower, in Glasgow. Here the
peak of seven per cent of the stock sold was in the very
'best' one per cent, and there was a plateau of relatively
high sales down to the 10-20 per cent category. Applying
Scottish LA/SSHA bands did little to change the position in
Edinburgh, though in Glasgow it did increase the rate in the
'best' one per cent to 11 per cent, and extended the plateau
of higher level sales down to the 30-40 per cent band. This
effect was due to the fact that relatively little of
Glasgow's stock qualified for the 'best' end of the Scottish
range. However, it is worth noting that, as with the new
towns, Edinburgh's higher overall level of sales extended
through all types of area and was thus not solely derived
from its relatively well-favoured stock.

Urban and Rural: Extending our consideration from Glasgow
to the Clydeside conurbation changes little. The plateau is
again in the 'best' 20 per cent of the stock, with sales
peaking at about one-twelfth in the 'best' one per cent.
Comparing this with the most rural areas of Scotland, we see
much more extensive sales, continuing at noticeable levels
right down to the 'worst' 10 per cent, though the peak level,
in the one to five per cent category was not much greater, at
one-ninth, than in the urban areas. This was partly due to
the relative lack of deprivation in rural Scotland, but, once
again, even comparing on a similar basis, the rural areas had
a higher level of sales right down almost to where they ran
out of stock.

Semi-detached or Terraced Houses and Low Rise Flats: There
was a lower level and stronger concentration of low rise
sales in the better stock, contrasted with a higher level and
more even spread of sales in the semi-detached and terraced
stock. This time, however, the peak rates were further
apart: only four per cent in the 'best' one to five per cent
of low rise stock, against 13 per cent in the best one per
cent semi-detached or terraced stock.

Conclusion: Generally speaking, the more deprived the stock
of an area was overall, the lower and more concentrated were
its level of sales. The evidence from both the Scottish and
local bandings indicates that higher selling areas sold more
not only because of their relatively well-favoured stock, but
also because of higher rates of sales in seemingly equivalent
areas of all qualities from the 'best' to the 'worst'. One
result of this wide distribution is that not even in some of

the highest selling districts (Stewartry and North East Fife) had more than about 15 per cent of the Scottish 'best' tenth of the stock been sold. It is difficult to explain this apparent limit on the level of sales of different areas, especially since the deprivation score concentrated on several of the factors which we might have expected to influence willingness or ability to purchase: for example, employment and earnings (through low SEGs). Perhaps the score misses out some important important factor, or maybe sales started off in the best areas and then worked outwards for some reason, though this would make more sense were the buyers not sitting tenants. Whatever the answer, it is clear that sales were not exclusively concentrated in the 'best' areas, and that the sale of one per cent, etc. of the stock did not necessarily mean that the 'best' one per cent, etc. had been sold Purchase was attractive to sitting tenants in a wide range of areas, and there is some time to go on present progress before even half of the 'best' areas have been moved from public to private ownership.

GENERAL CONCLUSION

We have looked at a number of measures of the contribution of sales to public sector change in Scotland, in order to assess whether the government's policy has had, or is likely to have, a major influence on the size, distribution and quality of the tenure. From the evidence it is clear that, though sales were potentially the biggest source of influence on these features, they had not reached the levels which would presage the imminent demise of the public sector in any part of Scotland. In fact it was extremely unlikely that the public sector would drop even to the current English and Welsh share in this century. The levels of sales which had been attained were also far from being spatially concentrated into powerful local effects at the most disaggregated level; rather sales tended to be spread around thinly and evenly. And, finally, though predominantly of the better types of property, the spread of sales through a wide range of different areas, 'good' and 'bad', meant that their effect was not concentrated on removing the 'best' parts of the public sector from the tenure. Sales in these areas had been higher, but they still remained, and probably would remain, substantially unaffected by the policy.

Chapter Seven

TRENDS IN HOUSING MANAGEMENT

David Clapham

The current trends in public sector housing
outlined in previous chapters have profound implications for
the management practices of local housing authorities and for
the role of professional housing managers. This chapter
explores the impact of these trends, which is important
enough to change the context within which housing management
has to operate and to provide a searching test of current
management methods. There is a growing unease both within
and outside the housing profession concerning the ability of
existing management practices to cope with the changing
situation. To understand the causes of this unease, it is
necessary to trace housing management back to the beginnings
of housing reform in the nineteenth century. The management
role can then be seen to be complex and multi-faceted, and to
give rise to debate about the emphasis which should be placed
on its component parts. Current trends in the public sector
have stimulated this debate and increased the urgency of the
search for coherent answers, but there appears, as yet, to be
little sign of agreement among the parties involved. The
debate has focused on three different views of the management
role: the 'contractual' role, the 'social' role and tenant
self-management. These are sometimes put forward as
conflicting views about the direction in which housing
management should be moving, although they are not
necessarily mutually exclusive except, perhaps, in their most
extreme forms. This is highlighted by the difficulty
experienced in defining the boundaries of the approaches in
theoretical terms and of finding actual examples which
involve only one approach. The discussion of these three
approaches does, however, shed some light on the possible
future direction of housing management.

THE MANAGEMENT STYLE OF LOCAL HOUSING AUTHORITIES

When the evolution of local authority housing
management is discussed the starting point is usually Octavia
Hill, that sterling Victorian woman who is often held to have

established modern housing management principles almost
single handed. The continuing influence of a woman who last
carried out housing work some 80 year ago is a testimony to
the importance of her contribution; but it is even more a
testimony to the paucity of thought which has since been
given to housing management, and to its lack of a coherent
role today.

Octavia Hill's work has been described many times
but some important points are relevant here (Hill, 1875;
Malpass, 1984; Moberly Bell, 1942). There was a close
relationship between Octavia Hill's housing work and social
work; indeed, they were really no more than different
aspects of the one activity. She was a founder member of
the London Association for the Prevention of Pauperisation
and Crime, the forerunner of the Charity Organisation Society
with which she was closely involved. The Charity
Organisation Society played an important role in establishing
the practice of social work, and Octavia Hill's method of
housing management shared with social work an emphasis on
personal contact with individuals and families. As Malpass
notes, 'the key to understanding her approach is that she
made housing management into a form of social work' (Malpass,
1984, p.34). She trained a large number of women housing
managers who went from house to house collecting rents and at
the same time building up a relationship with tenants. As
in social work this personal relationship was used as a means
of social control in an attempt to check inappropriate
behaviour such as drunkenness or sloth. The approach was
overtly authoritarian, as Octavia Hill admitted, but her
faith in the correctness of her values and of her duty to
impose them on others meant that she was rarely in any doubt
about the proper function of housing management. The
strength of her approach is that it provided a clear,
unambiguous model of housing management, and as such has
retained tremendous force. The influence of Octavia Hill's
model on modern local authority housing practice is, however,
a matter of some dispute. Malpass argues that when public
housing management became important after 1919, local
authorities adopted a very different model of management:

> Despite Octavia Hill's valuable pioneering work
> in this field, housing management was, in effect,
> reinvented in the 1920s as a wholly
> administrative activity centred on local
> government and lacking the moralistic overtones
> of her method (Malpass, 1984, p.36).

This statement is largely true in that, for most
local authorities, housing management was a bureaucratic,
impersonal, and functionally divided activity, often
involving a number of different departments, and usually
carried out by men. This was in sharp contrast to the few

108

local authorities which adopted the all-embracing approach of Miss Hill and employed women housing managers to work 'on Octavia Hill lines' (Brion and Tinker, 1980; Daunton, 1984).

However, in the 1930s the changing social role of public housing caused a widespread questioning of local authority housing management organisation and practice. During the 1930s the circumstances of households entering public housing began to change in that new property, instead of being let to the respectable working class or even the lower middle class as happened during the 1920s, was allocated to those who were being displaced by slum clearance programmes. The latter, for obvious reasons, were generally amongst the poorest of the working class. The problems this caused led to a debate about the proper role of housing management, in which the Society of Women Housing Estate Managers, an organisation formed by the followers of Octavia Hill, argued that local authorities should employ properly trained staff. The rival Institute of Housing Administration, formed in 1931 by predominantly male, local authority housing managers, saw a need for 'welfare work' among council tenants but argued that this should be kept separate from the largely administrative task of housing management. The differing views surfaced in evidence to the Central Housing Advisory Committee which undertook the first full-scale, government sponsored, investigation of housing management (CHAC, 1938). The report attempted to reconcile the two positions, although it argued that the personal approach to housing management was important and that welfare aspects should not be neglected. On the whole, however, the Octavia Hill school did not make a great deal of progress, and the rival associations merged in the 1960s to form what is now known as the Institute of Housing.

The result of this merger is that some aspects of the Octavia Hill model have been assimilated into local authority practice, although the key element of personal contact between manager and tenant has not been generally accepted. One example of a practice which can be traced back to Octavia Hill is the explicit grading of tenants, usually carried out by housing visitors whose assessment of a household's housekeeping standards has been used to determine the quality of accommodation offered (Damer and Madigan, 1974; Tucker, 1966). Another example is the use of onerous clauses in tenancy agreements. One local authority in Scotland still considers it necessary to forbid its tenants to keep coal in the bath. However, these practices are dying out, and therefore cannot be used as evidence of widespread acceptance of Octavia Hill's ideas. Local authority housing management has continued to be a largely administrative activity, in contrast to the personal, moralistic and authoritarian practices of Miss Hill.

However, as in the 1930s, the changing context of public housing is leading to problems with existing housing management methods. The Housing Research Group at the City University (1981), in an investigation of housing management in four local authorities, pointed to confusion as to the respective responsibilities of landlord and tenant, and also uncertainty as to whether housing management was to take on what they called a 'welfare role'. The result of this confusion was a lack of clear objectives in housing management and, therefore, of any means of assessing its performance. The outcome was a poor standard of service to tenants which was not helped by bad organisation. Local authority housing management was, therefore, shown to be inefficient and unsure of its role. Indeed, it has shown itself to be incapable of dealing with the situation which current trends affecting the public sector are creating; and it may even have contributed to these trends by adopting a management style which has endorsed the view of council housing as a second-rate tenure.

THE CHANGING CONTEXT OF HOUSING MANAGEMENT

There are two major trends, highlighted in previous chapters, which have implications for the management task of the housing authority: the changing nature and condition of the stock, and the changing social and economic characteristics of tenants.

It was stressed in chapters 5 and 6 that under the right-to-buy legislation it is the best properties which are being sold, predominantly houses with gardens in good locations, resulting in the public sector being left with only the less popular properties. This is occurring at a time when construction defects in much systems-built local authority property of the 1960s and 1970s are coming to the fore, as are problems with asbestos. The result is that many tenants are living in homes which are damp, difficult to heat and injurious to health. Added to this are problems of design and estate layout, which create oppressive and hostile environments. And local housing authorities are now having to come to terms with the age of some of their stock, particularly that built between the wars, much of which is still in urgent need of modernisation.

The state of repair of the stock is also unsatisfactory, constituting the biggest single complaint which tenants have about their housing, often stimulating the emergence of tenants' associations and providing a major rationale for the formation of management co-operatives. Repair problems have been exacerbated by an historic lack of maintenance of the stock, mainly because of the policy of merely responding to repair requests from tenants rather than regularly inspecting and maintaining property. Local authorities have traditionally had a repair rather than a maintenance policy. Even within the restricted confines of a repair policy, inefficiency in its operation has often

meant that the stock has deteriorated (National Consumer
Council, 1979). This has resulted in many housing
authorities facing increasing problems in keeping their stock
in a wind and water tight position, let alone ensuring that
it meets the needs and aspirations of tenants.

This situation has coincided with an unprecedented
squeeze by central government on spending on public housing,
as chapter 4 shows. The reduction in capital spending means
that major repairs, remedial work on structural defects, and
modernisation have been cut back. There has also been
pressure on housing revenue accounts from the reduction in
central government subsidy and the squeeze on rate fund
contributions. Coupled with high levels of arrears. this
has meant that lack of income has prevented necessary repairs
being carried out. Where local authorities have attempted
to make their repair systems more accessible to tenants, for
example through decentralisation, they have been overwhelmed
by the extra demand which has emerged. Therefore, as a
result of the sales policy, a legacy of an ageing and often
structurally unsound stock, central government restrictions
on capital expenditure, and the reduction of subsidies, local
housing authorities are being faced with increasing
management problems. They have much unpopular and
deteriorating housing and declining resources with which to
tackle these problems. In Glasgow, for instance, housing
managers are spending half of their time in processing
repairs, thus reducing the attention they can give to other
work. Sales are reducing rental income but the properties
left in the public sector are the most difficult to manage,
either because of their condition or because of their type,
for example deck access, tenement or multi-storey flats.

The changing social and economic status of tenants
has been charted in chapters 2 and 3. In summary, the
public sector is catering increasingly for the lower income,
and in some cases more dependent, groups in society: the
elderly, the long-term sick, the unemployed, one parent
families, ethnic minorities and the low paid. This trend
has profound implications for the local authority as
landlord, the most important of which is the growing
proportion of tenants living in poverty. The result is that
an increasingly large proportion of council tenants are
clients of more than one arm of the welfare state. The
arrears case of a housing assistant may also be a social
security recipient, a frequent user of health services or on
the caseload of a social worker. The problems of the tenant
are liable to cut across these professionally demarcated
service boundaries. Rent arrears may be caused by wrongly
calculated benefit payments, or recourse to health services
may be caused by bad housing conditions. Although the
tenant may basically only have one problem, many agencies can
be involved in its solution. Housing managers have found
themselves more and more involved with other social service

professionals, a fact which many have, as yet, to come to terms with satisfactorily.

The demands of groups with special housing needs, such as some of the elderly and the mentally and physically handicapped, have also forced housing managers into contact with other professionals. The 'community care' philosophy has increasingly meant that housing provision has been seen as the cornerstone of provision for these groups, and the public sector has been seen as playing a major role in this. The central government emphasis can be gauged by reference to the remit of the Scottish Special Housing Association (SSHA). Set up in 1937, the SSHA is a public body directly accountable to the Scottish Development Department and its work therefore closely reflects government priorities. The SSHA has been used to create employment in the 1930s, to provide overspill housing in the 1960s, and to contribute to inner city renewal in the 1970s, but since 1984 it has been largely restricted to catering for the special needs housing of the elderly and physically disabled. Most of new building by all public agencies is now for 'special needs'. Such provision involves local housing authorities in interaction with other welfare agencies such as the National Health Service and the personal social services. It involves consideration of the special needs of these groups in the physical design of housing, and also assessment of the physical and social capabilities of prospective tenants. This is essential in order to provide the right type of accommodation for each household, often including appropriate social support (such as a resident warden), with the result that housing departments have found themselves drawn into a more 'social' role. Sometimes this role is forced on them by a lack of integration of services; for example, people are discharged from psychiatric hospitals with nowhere to live and may find themselves approaching the local homeless persons unit. The increasing proportion of society's vulnerable groups who live in the public sector is putting increasing strain on housing management and posing a challenge which traditional methods are unable to meet.

These twin problems of a deteriorating stock and the changing social and economic status of tenants affect most of the public sector to some degree but the impact obviously varies from place to place. As pointed out in chapters 5 and 6, the right to buy is having a differential geographical impact and is exacerbating tenure differences between areas. Also, the impact of political and economic changes such as the increase in unemployment varies from one area to the next, and, as chapter 2 makes clear, these changes may also have a differential impact on local housing systems. Nevertheless, the direction of change for all or virtually all local housing authorities is the same, as are the resultant pressures, even if their weight may vary.

There is also a geographical dimension to the

incidence of the changes within particular local housing authorities which means that problems are concentrated in certain areas or estates. These are generally areas with the most unpopular and badly deteriorated housing which, because of the allocation system, is usually inhabited by the most deprived populations (Clapham and Kintrea, 1986), and which represent the residualised part of a residualised sector (Clapham and Maclennan, 1983). They are subject to stigma, contributing to an alienation from society often experienced by households in such areas, which can lead to a breakdown of informal social networks that control behaviour. As a consequence, a few people are able to dominate the community and to disrupt the lives of many. This is often exacerbated by bad design and layout of estates which encourage a feeling of alienation and a reluctance to get involved in anything outside one's front door (Coleman, 1985). For example, Seabrook (1984, p.11) notes that in Walsall the areas of the worst council housing are inhabited by the more vulnerable tenants.

> It has been interesting to observe that the departure of many of those who might have been community leaders has weakened the resistance to vandalism, petty crime, the many aggravations of daily life in the poor areas, the growth in some estates where there are a few black people of racism; the threat of violence, the break-up of so many families.

The breakdown of social order in these areas, and the high rates of poverty, vandalism and rent arrears, suggest that traditional methods of housing management are inadequate: they have failed to halt the decline and may indeed have contributed to it. This has caused unease among housing managers who are unsure of their own role in these circumstances, and it has brought to the fore the uncertainty and conflicts surrounding the management role in general.

The crisis in housing management is beginning to lead to a reappraisal of its role and to attempts to change existing practices through local experiments. However, no consensus has emerged and three different emphases are being pursued. The first approach stresses the contractual nature of the landlord-tenant relationship and seeks to distance housing management from a social role, whereas the second approach seeks to embrace that role more fully. The third approach seeks to devolve control over housing management to tenants themselves. Each of these three approaches will be examined in turn and some current developments in housing management will be found to illustrate how these models have informed current practice.

THE CONTRACTUAL APPROACH

Advocates of the contractual approach seek to remove housing management from the realm of social services by eliminating its 'social' objectives and, therefore, enabling it to concentrate exclusively on providing an efficient service to the generality of tenants. It is argued that the social service needs of individuals are the same whichever tenure they inhabit, and should be dealt with by the same social service agencies rather than by public landlords. In this way it is hoped that the paternalism and stigma currently inherent in public housing will be avoided.

> If public housing is ever to escape the stigma of welfare provision, the contractual nature of tenancy must be recognised. Although many council tenants receive other forms of social service and income maintenance from the local authority, this should not colour the specific relationship between landlord and tenant. It is based on a contract that is neither individually negotiable nor freely and equally entered upon, but its basis is still the payment of rent in return for the supply and maintenance of a home (Moseley, 1984, p.110).

The crux of this model is the improvement in the contractual relationship between landlord and tenant. It is argued that the breakdown of local authority management has occurred because of the lack of a clear exposition of the rights and duties of both landlord and tenant, and because of the poor service delivered by local authorities which they have been able to get away with only because of the lack of legal remedies available to tenants.

Advocates of this approach have concentrated attention on tenancy agreements between tenants and the public landlord, which have been criticised for being incomprehensible and loaded in favour of the landlord (Housing Research Group, City University, 1981). The Housing Act, 1980 and the Tenants' Rights, Etc. (Scotland) Act, 1980 obliged local authorities to publish their agreements and distribute them to all tenants, and ensured that changes in the agreement are negotiated with tenants. At the same time the acts gave additional rights to tenants, such as the right to security of tenure and to sublet. Although the provisions of the legislation were generally welcomed, the results have not assuaged the demand for more change. Tenancy agreements formulated after the 1980 legislation have been criticised as being paternalistic and difficult to understand (Scottish Consumer Council, 1983), and the package of rights given to tenants has been considered to be inadequate. In particular, tenants are held to have few rights over repairs to their houses. Some local authorities, such as Brent and Haringey have implemented their own repair schemes which formed the basis of the legislative proposals of the political parties. The government's proposals were contained in the Housing and Building Control Act, 1984, though the detailed provisions of the new 'right to repair' have been criticised as cumbersome.

Other campaigns have taken place in an attempt to improve the rights of tenants. One has concentrated on the value for money tenants receive from their rent. Examination of housing revenue accounts has uncovered the fact that tenants are often paying for some facilities in public housing areas, such as street lighting and sewers, through their rent as well as through their rates. Tenants' organisations have suggested the setting up of a landlord account to which only the cost of actual housing services provided to public tenants would be charged, excluding such items as street cleaning services, social support in sheltered housing or help to households in other tenures (Fielding, 1984). It is crucial to the contractual approach that there is a direct relationship between the rent paid and services received by tenants.

Concern has also been expressed about the lack of access to environmental health law by tenants because the local authority, through its environmental health department, might end up prosecuting itself as landlord. Access to the services provided by the local authority as landlord are also considered to be important. Decentralisation of housing management is, therefore, supported because of its beneficial effect on the efficiency of services rather than because of any conception of local democracy (Moseley, 1984).

The divorce between the landlord and welfare roles of local authorities is at the heart of this approach, and, because of the nature of local authorities as multiple providers of services, it calls into question whether they should be landlords at all. The divorce could be achieved more effectively if the functions were carried out by different bodies, but while local authorities remain as landlords it is difficult to see the split in functions working effectively. As was argued earlier, housing managers are being inexorably drawn into functions outside the narrow landlord role, whether through the recovery of rent arrears, the settlement of neighbour disputes, dealing with effects of vandalism, or the management of special needs housing. In the case of rent arrears it is in the interests of a housing authority to make sure that a tenant in arrears with the rent has advice on welfare benefits or advice on how to manage his or her household budget. The alternative, if the welfare role is eschewed, is the more frequent use of legal remedies such as eviction. A more formalised, contractual relationship may have some advantages in providing an efficient and easily understood system which could minimise accidental arrears for the tenant, but if housing authorities are stripped of their welfare functions they will, perhaps, be more likely to resort to legal remedies which could have disadvantages as well.

Tenants' problems are also not confined to a single service such as housing. A housing problem, an income problem and a personal social services problem may be symptoms of one underlying difficulty experienced by the tenant, for example marital breakdown, and the lack of a unified response may not be helpful to the tenant or the housing authority. In addition, the emphasis on a limited role for housing assistants can mean a chance to recognise social problems and to channel aid towards them is lost.

Improving the legal rights of tenants will undoubtedly both enhance their position vis-a-vis landlords and help to counteract some current trends. In particular, legal powers to ensure that properties are fit for occupation and kept in good repair could make a large difference to the deteriorating public stock, and could force central government and local authorities to make money available for this purpose. It is, however, difficult to see how a purely contractual approach could be maintained and how it would solve the social problems evident in some estates.

Advocates of the contractual approach have tended to see it as consisting of an individual relationship between the landlord and each tenant. But there is no reason why the contract should not be between the landlord and a collectivity of tenants or, where the tenants are also joint owners of the property, between them and the providers of management and maintenance services. An example of this kind of approach is the co-operatives in Norway and Sweden which appear to work very well (Clapham et al, 1985). This approach is really a variant of tenant self-management and will be discussed later. It does, however, serve to point out the difficulties in drawing a boundary between the different approaches.

THE SOCIAL ROLE OF HOUSING MANAGEMENT

Rather than trying to fight against the pressures pushing housing management into a more socially oriented role, some local housing authorities have reacted by accepting the need to adapt existing practices and to adopt a 'social' role. This can be seen as a return to the methods of Octavia Hill and a re-unification of housing management and social work. But neither point should be taken too far: present conditions demand a very different approach from that pursued by Octavia Hill, and nor is housing management likely to become a form of social work or even to draw more than inspiration from it. Rather, housing management is changing pragmatically to suit the circumstances in which it finds itself, and the effect of this is to draw it closer to other welfare professionals and to some current forms of social work practice.

The major focus of social work is on individuals and families. Housing managers are also becoming more involved at this level through dealing with families in rent arrears, and in coping with tenants who have special housing needs such as the mentally ill, mentally handicapped or physically disabled. Housing managers are either finding themselves in a position of providing advice on welfare benefits and social support to some tenants, or at least having to be able to refer them to other welfare professionals specialising in these fields.

Social work can also take a more community oriented approach, as encouraged by both the Seebohm (1968) and Barclay (1982) reports. The Barclay report claims that social work should consist of two main activities, individual counselling and what it calls 'social care planning'. This latter activity would involve the social worker in a social services department in planning, establishing, maintaining and evaluating the provision of social care, whether this care is provided by statutory agencies, voluntary agencies, families or other people in the community. An important part of this role is in promoting community networks.

> We also consider that the social services departments, through their social workers, have a responsibility for creating, stimulating and supporting networks in the community which may prevent the occurrence of some social problems and be available to help those who will have problems in the future (Barclay, 1982, p.43).

The Barclay report, therefore, places a strong emphasis on the concept of a 'community' and of social workers' role in relation to it, and it is this emphasis which housing management seems to be adopting. However, the concept of 'community' has been much criticised, not least by a prominent member of the Barclay committee, Robert Pinker. He argues that 'community' is impossible to define and contains false assumptions of a communality of interest among residents in an area. However, it is unlikely that housing managers working in difficult-to-let estates where this approach has mainly been used have any difficulty in knowing what the approach means in practice. A communality of interest is not difficult to find when physical, environmental and social conditions are as bad as they are in many areas of public housing.

If housing managers are to take on a more socially oriented role, organisational changes will have to be made. The scale of housing management will have to be reduced so that there is more personal contact between landlord and

117

tenant. Octavia Hill had an office in the blocks she was managing and used regular visits to collect the rent as a means of getting to know her tenants. This form of rent collection appears in many areas to be a thing of the past; therefore housing managers will, in order to build up personal relationships, have to spend more time on their 'patch' and be more accessible to tenants by being based in local offices. This will entail relieving housing managers of a good deal of the routine work which takes up so much of their time at the moment. The Housing Research Group of the City University (1981) suggests that there should be two types of housing manager, administrative assistants and tenancy officers. The former would carry out the majority of the routine activities of management, such as sending out standard arrears letters or ordering repairs, and would specialise in particular activities. This would leave the tenancy officer free to spend more time on his patch with tenants. A tenancy officer's role could be to monitor and evaluate the service provided to tenants, and also help to set up and maintain community networks; these would ensure the better functioning of the estate, the upkeep of common areas, and the provision of practical support for vulnerable families.

In coming to terms with a community centred role, housing managers will also have to accept the right of communities to determine their own destiny. Participation is therefore an integral part of the approach. The emphasis is on helping a community to mobilise its own resources. Housing managers would also have to come to terms with the social control aspects of the social role, and balance the needs and rights of the individual with the needs and rights of the community. Managers would have powers to apply for the eviction of tenants and have control over the allocation of tenancies. Octavia Hill was prepared to use such powers for what she saw as the good of the tenant and the community, and modern housing managers carrying out the kind of community function outlined here will also have to make decisions about their use.

The willingness to adopt a socially oriented role is shown by the increasing tendency for housing departments to employ community development workers, welfare rights specialists and even social workers. Where they are not employed in the housing department some local authorities have attempted to promote co-operation by combining offices at the local level or by pursuing joint initiatives to solve problems in particular estates. However, the approach has been put into practice more fully in the Priority Estates Project (PEP), which consists of a series of individual projects in different areas of England and Wales supported by the Department of the Environment with the aim of improving physical and social conditions in difficult-to-let estates. Although the projects vary considerably in their approach, they all share a commitment to locally-based, intensive management which is said to stem directly from the tradition of Octavia Hill, as the consultant to the PEP points out:

> The basic idea was not new or difficult: to establish a local management office, to carry out meticulously the landlord's responsibility for rent, repairs, letting property and maintaining the environment of the estate; and to give tenants a chance to exercise maximum control over their homes and neighbourhood. Octavia Hill in the nineteenth century pioneered this very approach in some of London's most scandalous slum tenements. Allowing for Victorian concepts of class and morality, her work in organising among tenants, and her tough but sensitive approach to housing management, proved a path-finder which the old-fashioned housing charities, such as the Sutton Housing Trust, have kept going to date (Power, 1984, p. 1).

The PEP approach differs from Octavia Hill's in that it is not overtly moralistic, it places more emphasis on the community model of social work than the individual one, and includes a commitment to tenant participation. Both approaches share a willingness to encompass social control, albeit with different emphases and a commitment to the meticulous performance of detailed management tasks, although in the PEP this is not conditional on the moral status of the tenant as it was with Octavia Hill.

The PEP approach has been very influential and has been applied by many local authorities to particular estates. In Walsall, which has decentralised many of its housing management functions to local offices, the PEP approach seems to be used in at least some of them. For example, Jeremy Seabrook (1984) documents the actions of one neighbourhood officer on the Goscote estate who saw his role as educating tenants to clean up their houses, collected the rent the day after benefits were paid in order to minimise arrears, and was tough on vandalism and other petty crime. The officer realised he could be criticised for being paternalist but he justified this approach on the grounds that the area had deteriorated so far that almost all tenants had lost hope and had given up trying to improve their position; when he arrived the tenants' association only had three members. He considered that a highly interventionist and paternalist approach was necessary to create the conditions under which tenants would want and be able to take control of their own housing.

Increasing tenant involvement was one of the objectives of the decentralisation initiative in Walsall. The aim was to involve tenants in decision-making about themselves, and to increase people's confidence to participate and make decisions. The emphasis on the need to ensure effective community functioning can, therefore, be seen as a stepping stone to enable communities to take over control of their neighbourhoods. It may also, however, in some circumstances be seen as an alternative to real control, giving tenants the feelings of having participated even if, in reality, decisions are made by housing managers.

There will undoubtedly be criticism of the paternalism involved in this new role. Critics will question the motives behind it and will wonder whether the objective is merely to 'police' tenants, and prevent them from protesting against poor conditions and creating trouble in the wider society. The PEP approach may also be seen as an alternative to the proper renovation of public housing. Octavia Hill provided minimal conditions in her housing and saw intensive management as avoiding expensive physical improvements which would put rents out of the reach of poor tenants. The PEP approach may be seen by some local authorities as a low cost way of dealing with problem areas, and PEP has gone to great lengths to stress the cost-effectiveness of its methods. It is, therefore, a very attractive approach for local housing authorities facing financial constraints.

If the new role for housing management is accepted, changes in training would be involved. Managers would need to have deeper understanding of social processes and a wider knowledge of other social services such as health, education and social security. The manager would have to know enough to be able to advise tenants about minor problems and be able to pass on those with more difficult ones to the relevant specialist.

The acceptance of a greater 'social' role for housing management might end the uncertainty which afflicts the profession. It is argued that the approach will improve service to tenants, with a wide range of needs and problems being dealt at one point. In addition, it could lead to the revitalisation of communities and the re-awakening of 'community spirit'. The experience of the PEP project appears heartening in all these respects, and it suggests that socially oriented housing management may often be the best way forward for both tenants and the profession.

TENANT SELF-MANAGEMENT

One answer put forward to the paternalism and inefficiency of local authority housing management has been, in effect, to abolish the landlord role and to enable tenants to manage their own housing. This approach is put forward by Colin Ward:

My own view is that the whole tragedy of
housing policy since local authorities first
became involved in the provision of housing,
has been that they have taken over the
landlord role, unaltered, from the private
landlord. The landlord-tenant relationship
has never been a happy one. In Britain it
has always been accompanied by mutual
suspicion, to which, when housing was
conceived as a public service rather than a
source of profit, was added the syndrome of
dependency and resentment that characterises
the council estate (Ward, 1974, p.2).

Tenant self-management is, therefore, seen as a
remedy for tenant inertia and the attitude of dependence
which are said to characterise other styles of management;
the aim is to encourage self-help and mutual aid. These
qualities would not only improve the physical and social
conditions of public housing but would also reduce the stigma
attaching to the sector and its residents; and they might
encourage the qualities which may help residents in other
spheres of life, for instance competing in the job market.
Some tenants' groups have started by gaining control over
their housing, through, for example, management
co-operatives; but they are now considering progression to
other activities such as setting up community businesses.
Current trends in public housing make the achievement of
self-management easier in some ways but more difficult in
others. As an increasingly disadvantaged group,many tenants
are likely to have less self-confidence, to be resigned to
their situation and to lack leadership abilities. At the
same time, the many tenants who are prevented from making a
contribution to the wider society, for example the unemployed
and the retired, have time and energy to spare which many of
them are willing to devote to their local area. However, in
the places where current trends are felt most, the
difficult-to-let estates, tenants would be unlikely to want
to take over control of the estates, especially those with
major repair problems. Anne Power obviously supports the
principle of tenant control on PEP estates but concludes:

But many tenants are reluctant to assume such
wide responsibility, especially on estates
with multiple problems as in the present
sample. On only one of the 200 estates were
tenants contemplating establishing a
management organisation under their own
control. Even there it was only partial
(Power, 1984, p.37).

Tenant self-management is often criticised because of its neglect of wider interests than those of the current tenants of an area. This criticism is usually directed at allocation procedures. Undoubtedly one of the reasons that tenants may wish to control the management of their property is to be able to choose their neighbours. The concern is expressed that this will lead to ethnic minorities or so-called problem families being excluded. There is, therefore, pressure on local housing authorities to place constraints on tenant control by, for example, retaining rights over a proportion of lettings. This means that, in practice, tenant control is rarely absolute. Many functions, most importantly over the provision of financial resources, are often left with the housing authority, so that the authority may be open to charges of manipulation. John Turner (1972), a committed advocate of resident control, argues that deficiencies and imperfections in your housing are infinitely more tolerable if they are your responsibility than if they are somebody else's. The opportunity for the manipulation of tenants by local housing authorities is obvious, and this highlights the need for tenants to have effective control over important functions coupled with the resources to carry them out.

The most common form of tenant self-management is the management co-operative, several of which have been formed on existing local authority estates. The Cloverhall Estate in Rochdale was selected as one of the local examples of PEP, but the tenants decided at an early stage that they wanted to control management of the estate themselves and attempted to form a management co-operative. The tenants are now employing their own full-time worker and have negotiated a management agreement with the council (Power, 1984).

The Whiterose co-operative in the East End of Glasgow signed its agency agreement with Glasgow District Council in early 1983. The co-operative was formed by tenants dissatisfied with the allocation and repair policies of the council, who determined to manage the properties themselves. They now control repairs and run an allocation system. The members of the co-operative are undoubtedly pleased with their new status although they recognise that there are still problems. The most important one appears to be their continuing financial dependence on the district council which sets and collects rents, and pays a management and maintenance allowance. Any surpluses can be spent on improvements to the estate. The service which the co-operative can offer to its members depends crucially on the amount of the allowance which is the subject of yearly negotiations between the co-operative and the council. The co-operative is also dependent on the council for major repairs to the property, which at present is badly in need of modernisation.

Criticism could be levelled at the co-operative's allocation policy which restricts 70 per cent of the lettings to close relatives of existing members, although they do have to be on the council waiting list. The form of the policy has been dominated by the fact that 70 per cent of the existing tenants are pensioners, many of whom wish to have young relatives living close to them. The result would be a more balanced community and better social support for the elderly residents, but there is bound to be criticism of a policy which is so little related to housing need. This has led many councils to restrict the powers of co-operatives by insisting on nomination rights. The limited powers given to management co-operatives mean that they fall short of the ideals of advocates of resident control such as John Turner. He argues that 'tenants of public housing must have the right to run their own housing - that is, a right to the material as well as the social benefits of doing so - not just the dubious privilege of doing the council's work for them' (Turner, 1981, p.30).

Turner's ideal, therefore, is for tenants to be given the total control over their housing including a financial stake in their properties by taking on a share in the equity. But this raises interesting questions about whether or not such a form of tenure can be considered as public housing at all.

The assumption of control by tenants determines who manages the housing but it does not determine the style of management. Research is needed to ascertain what management style does evolve in this situation. Ward (1974) implies that tenants themselves are more likely to take on a welfare role and to take a hard line on anti-social behaviour. Whatever the management style, the assumption of control by tenants means a different role for the professional housing managers who are employed by them. Their professional autonomy is diminished as they become accountable to the tenants, and they see the area of work designated as 'professional' decrease as tenants perform more functions for themselves.

THE FUTURE OF HOUSING MANAGEMENT

The three approaches outlined here serve to highlight the different emphases which housing management can adopt. Although their advocates tend to see them as distinct and separate, it is difficult to draw firm boundaries between them, and practical developments rarely involve just one of these elements. Housing management is complex and encompasses many roles, some of which are conflicting but many of which are not mutually exclusive. Charting the future direction of housing management is, therefore, not a question of predicting which of these elements will prevail over the others but of seeing how the emphasis will shift between and within them.

Some recent developments, such as decentralisation of housing management, do tread common ground between the approaches, although the objectives attached to each initiative, and therefore the criteria used to assess its success or failure, differ. For example, advocates of the contractual approach would stress the objective of improving service delivery and physical access for tenants, whereas advocates of the social approach are more likely to stress the potential for personal contact between housing managers and tenants. Advocates of tenant control are likely to stress the potential of decentralisation in furthering this aim. The fact that decentralisation is supported by all of these groups is at the same time a strength and a weakness; it may be more likely to be implemented but its objectives are likely to be confused and conflicting. Reducing the scale of housing management does not remove the need to determine the style of management.

In order to foresee the direction in which housing management will move it is necessary to look again at the context of public housing and the current trends in its provision. As was outlined earlier, the sector is faced with a declining financial base, a deteriorating stock, an increasingly disadvantaged group of tenants, and a central government which sees it as being, at least eventually, provision of last resort. These factors are already forcing housing managers to adopt a more socially oriented approach, and this development is being supported by a government anxious to see the public sector come to terms with its envisaged role as a sector catering solely for 'social cases'. However, because of the differential spatial impact of current trends, the social approach is not likely to be uniformly applied; it will rather be concentrated in those areas with the worst problems. Also, this move is not likely to be the only direction of change. The acceptance of the social role may trigger off reactions from tenants' and political groups. In particular, the danger of the social role in leading to an erosion of the rights of individuals and an increase in social control may lead to growing pressure from tenants' associations for more contractual rights to provide a safeguard. In addition, some tenants may take advantage of the increased autonomy of locally-based housing management units and the improvement in social conditions which the social role may bring to take over more control of their housing by, for example, forming management co-operatives. The number of tenants' groups likely to take this option would seem to be small, particularly as the deteriorating state of the stock, which is unlikely to be checked by innovative management methods, means that they would be shouldering a considerable burden. Rather than taking on overall control, tenants' groups are likely to try to influence decentralised management units in order to tackle the particular problems in their local areas. This is likely to lead to a diversity of practice between areas and perhaps pave the way for innovation at the local level. Therefore, although housing management will begin to take on more fully a social orientation, this is likely to be combined with increasing pressure for improvements in tenants' rights and more diversity of practice at the local level.

It is evident, therefore, from the failure of traditional management structures and methods to deal with the current situation facing public housing that change is essential. Furthermore, these changes are likely to emerge as tenants and housing managers attempt to deal with a situation which is becoming increasingly intolerable for both. But the changes referred to in this chapter represent developments or extensions of the traditional landlord-tenant relationship in public housing. However, the pressures on the sector are so acute that, as chapter 9 shows, increasingly more radical changes are being discussed and implemented, such as the formation of housing trusts. These could herald the break up of the public sector in its present form and a radical reduction in the role of local authorities as landlords. Unless changes in managerial style and organisation are made soon, this break up may become increasingly attractive to tenants and many housing managers, as well as to central government which has shown itself keen to reduce local authority involvement in housing provision.

Chapter Eight

THE DECLINING FORTUNES OF SOCIAL RENTED HOUSING IN EUROPE

Michael Harloe

There are few European countries in which social
rented housing plays as large a role in housing provision as
it does in Britain; indeed in most of the poorer southern
European countries and several of the richer northern ones it
has no more than a minimal existence (for recent information
on southern Europe see Wynn, 1984). But there are a
relatively small number of states in which it does play a
much more important role, for example Sweden, Denmark, the
Netherlands, West Germany and France. This chapter
discusses the development and some of the current problems of
the tenure in such countries. It is based on research which
has been carried out by the author and Maartje Martens into
the development of housing markets and policies in Britain
and the last four of the five countries listed above (see
Harloe, 1981, 1984; Harloe and Martens, 1984, 1985;
Martens, 1985).

While there are many significant differences in the
current national circumstances of social housing, there are
many ways in which these circumstances, and the major
problems and policy dilemmas to which they give rise, are
broadly similar. Before discussing these central issues we
shall sketch out some of the more important ways in which
this tenure is rather differently constituted elsewhere in
comparison with Britain.

SOCIAL HOUSING: SOME NATIONAL DIFFERENCES

In Britain the distinction between private rented,
public rented and owner-occupied housing is still fairly
clear, despite the growth of so-called new forms of tenure in
recent years. In several other European countries this
simple division is less applicable. Here, the British model
of direct local authority provision is rare, at least on any
significant scale. A far more common pattern is for most
social housing to be owned and operated by a variety of
non-profit organisations, including housing associations and
co-operatives. This institutional difference has some

consequences.   In Britain, where the current prominence of
housing associations is almost wholly a product of recent
government promotion and subsidies, the extent to which the
associations can operate with any degree of autonomy is
severely limited.   In many other European countries which
have a significant social housing sector the non-profit
housing organisations have been the main vehicles for social
housing provision for a much longer time.   In Britain the
late nineteenth century experiments in philanthropic housing
provision were wholly abortive, and the organised working
class struggled for subsidised housing to be provided by the
local authorities.   But elsewhere housing co-operatives and
associations became the main focus for both working class and
middle class housing reform movements.

While the significance of these differences should
not be over emphasised, especially now when in every country
non-profit housing is heavily dependent on government
promotion and finance, the relatively greater independence of
the non-profit sector outside Britain, and the effectiveness
of the various national social housing federations in
lobbying for their interests and in resisting governmental
attempts to control their activities, do have some practical
consequences.   While these cannot be analysed here they can
at least be illustrated.   Thus, despite the current Dutch
government's apparent interest in following the British
example and initiating a policy of selling off social
housing, a major obstacle to any such policy is the long
established, widely accepted and legally underwritten formal
independence of the associations from either local or
national political control (Harloe and Martens, 1985).   More
generally, the autonomy of the non-profit landlords in Europe
has been evident in the widespread inability of either
central or local government to impose their own priorities on
the selection of tenants by these bodies.   Thus, in France
in the 1950s, the government wished to expand social housing
provision in order to accommodate key workers in the new and
expanding industries which lay at the heart of the country's
post-war economic regeneration.   But it was forced to
establish new bodies to carry out this policy because the
existing social housing organisations resisted a
reinterpretation of their role (Harloe, 1984).   More
recently, there is evidence from several countries of
continuing conflict between local authorities, which have
duties to obtain housing for those in severe social need, and
the non-profit bodies, which are the main suppliers of such
housing.   While research is almost non-existent, it is
evident that in such circumstances discrimination in letting
practices against low-income households, 'problem' families,
ethnic minorities and others is probably even more pervasive
than in Britain.

These institutional differences derive from the
particular nexus of economic, political and ideological

factors which surrounded the emergence of social rented housing in each country (see Harloe, 1981). This is too broad a topic to be comprehensively explored here, but there are two further important differences which do have to be noted. The first concerns the nature of the political support for social housing. In Britain, as Duclaud-Williams (1978) has noted, there has been a fairly clear cut 'politics of tenure' throughout much of the history of social housing. Overwhelmingly it is the Labour Party which has been seen, and has seen itself, as the main supporter of social housing, while the Conservative Party has sought to stem (and now to reduce) the size of this tenure. While the association of organised labour with social housing is important, elsewhere there has been support for social housing from non-socialist parties too. This is particularly evident in countries such as the Netherlands and West Germany where religious as well as class forces have helped form the party systems, and where 'pure' conservative parties have been less important than Catholic or Christian Democrat parties. Such parties have sought to appeal to working class voters, and they have incorporated 'workerist' sections pressing for social reform and for the expansion of welfare provision - including the development of social housing. So the institutional independence of the social housing sector has been bolstered by the fact that it has often been able to draw on some political support whatever government was in office. (The fact that in countries with systems of proportional representation coalition government has been the norm has also meant that pro-social housing interests are rarely absent from government.)

A final important area of difference concerns the varying post-war economic development of the European nations and its impact on national systems of housing provision. In 1945, Britain had long since made the transition to an industrially based, highly urbanised society. While both the housing stock and the economy were obsolescing, there was a relatively adequate quantity of housing and a relatively high level of per capita income. The war had left a legacy of severe problems but at least the wartime destruction of the economy and of the housing stock was fairly limited. The immediate belief was that future housing needs would mainly be met by the public sector. But, with the benefit of hindsight, it is easy to appreciate that, when the Conservative governments of the 1950s embarked on a policy of the expansion of owner occupied housing, the economic, political and social preconditions for this policy were all present. But conditions were very different elsewhere. First, few countries - with the exception of pre-war Germany - had attained Britain's level of economic development. In countries such as France, Denmark and the Netherlands there were still large rural sectors and heavy concentrations of small-scale business and industry. These were countries with low wages and relatively underdeveloped economies. In every case the following decades saw the rapid and successful rectification of this situation. But this resulted in rapid urbanisation, and a continuous and heavy demand for new housing, during a period when, for many years, incomes remained relatively low. The requirement for subsidised rented housing was, for economic and social reasons, rather high, not just for less skilled manual workers, but for a much wider section of the population. In Germany and the Netherlands, too, the extensive destruction of the pre-war stock added greatly to this demand. In France the economic stagnation in the inter-war period meant that the stock that survived the war was on average very old and highly defective, thus adding a further factor to the acuteness and urgency of the post-war housing problem. A consequence of this situation and its persistence for many years was that most governments, regardless of their ideological persuasion, had little option but to expand subsidised rental housing provision. Economically this was imperative if attempts to modernise relatively low wage economies were to succeed. Politically it was necessary as large sections of the electorate demanded such housing.

Having stressed the linked political and economic reasons for the expansion of subsidised rented housing, it must also be underlined that such expansion did not necessarily take the form of subsidised social rented housing - at least not exclusively. Governments such as those in Germany and France, which in principle supported the expansion of the private provision of housing, made 'social' subsidies available for private and non-profit landlords (and for owner occupation too, although for the reasons already stated this sector was slower to develop than in Britain). Nevertheless, in such countries the opportunity that British Conservative governments had to align housing policies with their ideological preferences was far less evident for much of the post-war period. Whether they liked it or not, continuing support for social rented housing long remained an important part of housing policy, regardless of the parties in government. (For a more detailed discussion of the issues raised in the last two paragraphs see Harloe, 1984.)

The purpose of this section of the chapter has been to sketch out some of the more important factors which have served to ensure that the social housing sector in a number of European countries is rather differently situated in their national housing systems in comparison with that in Britain. While in some cases these differences were more evident a decade or more ago than now and have been eroded by common economic, political and social developments, they are by no means insignificant for the current state of this sector in Europe. To summarise, it seems that the long established relative autonomy of non-profit housing, the lack of a clear cut 'politics of tenure', and the persisting social and economic rationale for such housing combined to bolster the sector's ability to resist - to a degree at least - the political and social marginalisation of the tenure. This process has been a slowly, but now more rapidly, emergent feature of council housing in Britain from the 1960s, and arguably the 1950s, onwards. Nevertheless, while what can only be described as the decline of social rented housing may have been less precipitous in other countries than in Britain, this difference appears now only to be a matter of degree, reflecting a slower development of the tenure's marginalisation rather than its absence. This is because the economic, political and social factors which resulted in marginalistion in Britain have become ever more evident elsewhere. We now turn to a brief examination of some of these factors.

CAUSES OF DECLINE

Successive reports of the Housing, Building and Planning Committee of the UN Economic Commission for Europe (ECE) provide the most complete overview of the changing fortunes of social rented housing in Europe (UN Economic Commission for Europe, 1949, 1954, 1958, 1973, 1976, 1980). What follows relies heavily on these reports. Most interestingly they show that the origins of some of the major problems which now beset social rented housing stretch back many years. The early post-war reports stress the enormous demand for new housing which then existed. This demand was in fact underestimated at 14 million dwellings in 1949 because of the failure to predict the demographic and locational developments which later occurred (the trend to smaller households, 'bulges' in the birth rate and the impact of economic development and urbanisation). In seeking to meet this demand, in circumstances where some action was essential but where financial, material and manpower resources were in short supply, certain policies were generally initiated which have had important long-term consequences. For example, many governments promoted considerable innovation in building techniques, especially low and high rise industrialised building. Also, many governments reduced space and other standards in the 1950s in order to maximise output (as did the British government with its 'people's house' in the early part of the decade). These measures, while they may have cheapened and speeded up production, have now resulted in high maintenance costs and an increasing amount of disrepair. In addition, much of the housing was built to space and other standards (for example, thermal and acoustic insulation, heating and ventilation) which are now regarded as inadequate, and on estates which suffer from various forms of environmental and social deprivation. Rising inner city land costs, brought about in part by economic growth and urbanisation, meant that land costs also became a major concern; in attempts to economise, peripheral sites were often used for the development of large scale estates of social housing. As in Britain these peripheral estates suffered because of their isolation from urban labour markets and services.

The second major problem concerns the economics of social housing. Difficulties began to be experienced in the early 1950s, although unlike the quality problems, which have only come to the fore in the past few years as the stock has aged and as its deficiencies have become clear, governments very rapidly began to express their concern. Thus by 1953 the ECE committee was questioning the heavy financial commitments of governments which had involved themselves in the long-term future support of social housing. There were two aspects to this. The first concerned the provision of large-scale public loans. As private capital markets revived, most governments - led by West Germany and Britain - reduced their commitment to these in favour of subsidising commercial loans. The second problem, the escalating costs of these subsidies, was more persistent. An important element in this escalation was the consequence of one of the major differences between the operation of social housing in Britain and elsewhere. In Britain rent pooling had been established in the mid-1930s but in most other countries it was not thought desirable or necessary for many years. Indeed, it was often specifically prohibited. In any event the independent status of the non-profit organisations, as well as the proliferation of these mainly small-scale providers of housing, would have made governmental insistence on rent pooling difficult and probably rather ineffective (organisations with small and mainly rather new stocks of housing had little housing built at low historic costs, so the redistribution to be obtained by pooling would have been very modest). In many cases the management of the non-profit organisations was heavily influenced or even controlled by the existing tenants who had little obvious reason to accept higher rents in order to cross-subsidise the rents of tenants moving into the newly built stock.

This meant that, especially when inflation accelerated from the 1960s onwards, it was necessary to provide increasingly deep subsidies if new housing was to be within the means of those who required it. At the same time, inflation and income growth meant that many existing tenants were paying very small proportions of their incomes in rent. In fact, in countries such as Germany and France, when governments tried to control the levels of subsidies for new building, the resulting rent levels meant that many households in housing need refused to accept such housing. Especially in the early 1970s, there was a growing stock of vacant and unlettable new social housing, and evidence that the non-profit organisations were increasingly using ability to pay as one of the criteria for access. While such problems have not been entirely absent in Britain, they have been less evident here than elsewhere. However, it is worth noting that this discrimination in favour of middle income households (together with the widespread resistance to housing 'problem' families, etc., noted earlier) has meant that, in some cases, European social housing has not become as exclusively occupied by economically, politically and socially 'marginal' groups as it often has in Britain.

In response to these problems many European governments have attempted to 'harmonise' rents, that is to raise the rents of older units and establish systems of rent setting which relate rents more closely to housing quality. In addition, from the 1960s onwards governments have moved away from 'object' (that is building) subsidies towards 'subject' subsidies (housing allowances). At first these allowances were seen as complementing more 'efficient' production subsidies, but in the last decade or so they have gradually become the main means by which many governments propose to subsidise social housing. These changes will be discussed in more detail later in the chapter.

In 1980 the ECE committee published its latest review of European housing. In some respects this document, quite naturally, reflects the experiences of the early 1970s, when the economic and political climate was very different from what it is now, and when many believed that the era of large-scale housing problems was at an end. But the report does show that some of the problems of the social housing sector were beginning to become quite acute. In many countries the production of this housing had peaked in the mid to late 1960s, but the high level of output came to an abrupt end with the first major symptom of the coming international economic crisis - the oil price rises of 1973. Even before this time, as already noted, there had been a growth of vacant new social rented housing in countries such as Denmark, West Germany, the Netherlands and Sweden. As also noted, the problem of high rents had contributed to this result (as well as the growth of owner occupation). While effective demand for these units was declining (and hence, it could be argued, there had been overproduction) there was plenty of evidence that there were still many groups in housing need. Groups such as the elderly, one parent families, the young, the disabled, ethnic minorities/guest workers and, generally, those with low earnings and/or dependent on state benefits still required affordable social housing.

As in Britain, though with far less impact and often reluctantly, some social housing organisations had turned towards the rehabilitation of older buildings and away from new building. (The resistance to this change of role reflects the independence of the social housing organisations and their lack of a legal responsibility for general housing conditions in their areas of operation, unlike British local

authorities.)   Towards the end of the 1970s, as the economic
situation again worsened with the growth of mass
unemployment, continuing inflation and severe pressures to
reduce public expenditure, there were in many countries, as
in Britain, more decisive moves by governments to withdraw
from subsidising new social rented housing, to reduce object
subsidies for existing units (relying ever more heavily on
housing allowances to deal with high individual housing
costs), and to place reliance on (subsidised) owner
occupation to meet future housing needs.   The growth of the
latter tenure was especially noticeable in countries such as
Denmark, Sweden, the Netherlands and West Germany, where
demand for rented housing had remained at a higher level than
in Britain through most of the post-war years.   Although
some may see the development of owner occupation in such
countries as an automatic consequence of their growing
prosperity, the facts are that this development was strongly
promoted by governments and by the major economic interests
involved in the private housing industry.   In fact towards
the end of the decade and in the early 1980s the private
housing market was itself in a severe slump, not unnaturally
given the general economic circumstances.   But this did not
lead to a revival in social rented housing.   While some
governments remained committed in theory to this tenure
(notably the socialist government in France), in practice the
overriding desire to control the growth of public expenditure
meant that new building remained at a low level, and the
strategy of reducing general subsidies and relying on housing
allowances persisted.   In several countries these policies
were more enthusiastically adopted - as in Britain - by right
wing governments which were ideologically committed to
expanding the private market in housing.   Given the vast
improvements in the housing conditions of the majority which
had occurred in the post-war decades and the growth of owner
occupation, the earlier political pressures for an expansion
of social housing were by now not nearly as strong as they
had been in the 1950s and 1960s.   Nor were there any longer
the economic reasons for such provision.   Just as there has
been a fading of the earlier consensus on the need to expand
the welfare state generally, so there has been a fading of
the constituency for social housing.   In fact, as in
Britain, social housing expenditure has commonly been the
first and one of the most severely affected victims of public
expenditure cuts.   Services such as education and health
which still benefit the majority of the population have been
able to resist cuts relatively more effectively than social
housing which only caters for a minority, and a minority
which is increasingly composed of groups which are marginal
in both economic and political terms.   While this
development is most apparent in Britain, it characterises
many other European countries too.

This section has outlined some of the major factors which have begun to result in social housing being confined to a residual role in even the relatively few European countries, such as Sweden, Denmark, the Netherlands, West Germany and France, where the tenure had expanded substantially up to the 1970s. Within this increasingly restricted tenure there are several major problem areas which housing policy is now focusing on. The three that are found in virtually every country concern subsidies and rents, housing quality and housing management. The sale of social rented housing is not yet nearly so important an issue as it has been in Britain since 1980, although it is likely to emerge as a major concern in West Germany over the next few years and possibly in the Netherlands as well. In the next sections of the paper we shall discuss these issues in more detail.

SUBSIDIES AND RENTS

The general background to these issues has already been noted - the movement from production to consumption subsidies accompanied by higher rent levels, the pressure to restrict public expenditure and the general impact of inflation. But there are other important considerations too. First, there have been very rapid rises in costs due to two elements which are particularly important in the case of housing - land prices and interest rates. Second, there is the problem of the stagnant or declining real incomes of the low and moderate income households which increasingly predominate in the social sector. Especially with the rise in unemployment, the issue of the affordability of social housing has grown in importance.

One of the main responses to the rising subsidy bill was the introduction of degressive construction subsidies, that is subsidies which reduce over time as, it is assumed, tenant incomes and hence ability to pay increase. This strategy was adopted in Denmark in 1966 and has also been used in the Netherlands, Sweden, West Germany and France. The problem has been that such schemes have to make assumptions about future movements in costs and incomes, and these have often proved to be false (normally being rather too optimistic). In these circumstances governments have had to consider whether to step in and 'bail out' such schemes with additional subsidies, as occurred, for example, in Denmark and the Netherlands (for further details see Priemus, 1981). The alternative outcome has been that which was outlined by a senior West German housing official; writing in 1975 he noted that, when taken in combination with sharp increases in operating costs (due, as elsewhere, to energy price and wage rises) and interest rates, the predetermined decreases in subsidies resulted in very high rent increases (Pfeiffer and Stahl, 1975). These caused considerable hardship to some tenants and a reduction in the affordability of new units for many of those who required them. The fact is that degressive subsidies work best when the inflation with which they aim to deal is accompanied by full employment and growing personal incomes. This was the situation in the 1960s and early 1970s when such schemes began (and of course it was the situation which greatly encouraged the expansion of owner occupation). But today the continuing increase in the cost of housing is not accompanied, at least among those groups of the population which most require social housing, by rising real personal incomes. We shall return to the problems which this poses for current and future policies in the last section of the chapter.

Of course the problem of individually high rent/income ratios under the new regimes of 'harmonised' rents and degressive subsidies was supposed to be met by the expansion of housing allowances. Such schemes, which hardly existed at all before the 1960s, subsequently expanded in coverage - and cost - very greatly. As developments in Britain have followed a very similar pattern, as the limitations of such schemes do not vary greatly from country to country, at least in their fundamentals, and as there has probably been more research and discussion of these problems in Britain than in any other European country, we shall not consider these schemes in detail (for useful discussions see Howenstine, 1975, 1983). Some countries do have systems which are more problematic in certain respects than others; for example, in West Germany the maximum allowable rent has often been far less than the cost related rents of new social housing, while elsewhere it is more normal for the full rent to be accepted for the purposes of allowance calculations. But limited take-up of benefits, problems of maximum permissable rents for the purposes of the allowance calculation, and the limits of allowances as a means of supporting new building are all widely encountered.

However, there are two further matters which seem to be becoming more significant as the concentration of lower income households in the rented sector has grown and as rents have risen sharply. The first concerns the assumptions which these schemes make about the proportion of income which households are able to pay towards their own housing costs. Few schemes adequately recognise that low income households can often only afford to pay a much lower proportion of their incomes for housing than other households. The second issue concerns the administrative costs of this form of subsidy which are high. When allowance schemes began it was commonly the case that rather few tenants benefitted from them and expenditure on administration was relatively low. Today many more tenants benefit from these schemes and the administrative costs have risen greatly. Linked to this is the more important issue of the net benefit to governments, in terms of subsidy savings, from these administratively costly schemes. When rents were relatively low, object subsidies extensive and incomes growing rapidly, there were major savings to be made by moving from universal to selective subsidies. The net gain from further increases in rents, withdrawal of general subsidies and extension of individual allowances is now far less; see chapter 4 for the British experience. In short, the general strategy which has been pursued is beginning to show diminishing returns.

A final point is that, faced with the impossibility of extending further the cuts in construction subsidies which have already been made - partly because some minimal social housing construction is still required and partly because, after the major cuts of the last few years, there is anyway often little more to be gained from this source in terms of expenditure savings - several governments have followed or are contemplating following the British government's recent policy of beginning to stem the growth of personal subsidies. If successful these changes are bound to have a severe impact on many of those now living in social housing.

THE QUALITY OF SOCIAL HOUSING

Reference has already been made to the modest standards of much of the social housing built in the 1950s as well as to the spread of industrialised building. In the 1960s, as available resources and incomes expanded, most countries raised the standards of new construction by increasing the size of units, providing central heating and so on. But the 1960s also saw the acceleration of industrialised construction which lowered rather than raised the structural quality of new housing, and has required frequent and costly maintenance expenditure. So, despite the improvement in matters such as internal facilities and space, it is very difficult to sustain the claim that the overall quality of the new social housing estates was necessarily greater than it had previously been.

By the 1970s two things became clear. First, the new building techniques had left an expensive legacy for the future. Second, the increasing standards of space, heating and other amenities had added considerably to the rapid inflation of building costs which had occurred. Increasingly, the question of the affordability of these standards has come to the fore, and there are now widespread moves to re-examine and reduce the standards which were previously in force. In Britain the present government has abandoned the Parker Morris standards in favour of a 'value for money' standard. In the Netherlands there has been an extensive examination of how economies might be gained by reducing 'non essential' standards. In Germany, where the problem of high standards and costs is acute, there has also been a move towards minimal rehabilitation by social housing organisations. These moves mirror similar developments in the private sector which have been occurring in face of the problem of the affordability of new housing for first time buyers. So far there do not seem to have been any great savings gained by the attempts to reduce 'non essential' standards. In the private sector the most significant economy seems to be obtained by reductions in land costs via increased housing densities. In the social sector, where densities already tend to be high (and where they have often been heavily criticised for being too high), this form of saving is much less possible. Anyway, at a time when the deterioration of much of the social rented stock is a growing problem, most governments appear to be concerned not to reproduce past mistakes by any substantial reduction of basic construction standards; yet this is where the greatest savings could potentially be made, at least in the short run.

The problem of the deterioration of extensive areas of social rented housing, especially that located on high density, industrially built estates is of major concern in most European countries (see Wynn, 1984). The causes of this deterioration are complex and far from wholly understood. They involve not only the physical attributes of the housing but also the demographic and social composition of its inhabitants. While there would in any case have been a growing need for the rehabilitation of social housing by the 1980s owing to the normal deterioration of buildings, many of which are now over 30 years old, what has given rise to far greater concern, and will cost far more to rectify, is the very rapid deterioration of many of the units built between the late 1950s and the early 1970s. Not only are these units often very costly to repair because they have serious building and design faults and because their industrialised construction makes them more difficult to rectify, but generally they are still in receipt of construction subsidies. Moreover, the defects tend to add greatly to operating costs (for example heating costs) for the authorities and tenants. The problems of these areas are not simply confined to the structures, for the layout of many of these estates has come under increasing criticism. Features such as deck access and the lack of private open space are often unpopular with tenants, provide a great deal of 'indefensible space', and are extremely costly to improve, if indeed this is possible at all.

In addition, there is often a complex intertwining of physical and social problems. There tends to be a vicious circle in which progressive deterioration and the growth of social problems mutually reinforce each other. The exact nature of this relationship and its progress varies, but among the links commonly recognised are the following:

1.   Physical deterioration, leading to the progressive downgrading of the acceptability of the estate to many actual or potential tenants.   This tends to result in rising vacancy rates, and the vacant units often become vandalised leading to further withdrawal of tenants.

2.   The tendency which seems universal for social housing landlords to use such areas as 'sink' estates for housing 'problem' tenants, thus reinforcing the social stigmatisation of such areas and often resulting in further vandalism and withdrawal.   This has often been made worse by the policies of minimal maintenance which have been followed in such areas.

3.   More generally, management practices have often added further dimensions to the problems of these areas.   In particular, as in Britain, discriminatory practices in housing allocation have resulted in high concentrations of ethnic minorities and/or guest workers in some areas.   In societies where racism is endemic this has contributed to the growth of intergroup tension and, in France for example, episodes of open and even violent conflict.   Other management practices have also had adverse effects.   For example, the increasing use of centralised, computerised rent collection and centrally based caretaking and repair services, while in the short run possibly saving management costs, have often resulted in poorer services to tenants and a less constant and effective management presence in the housing areas.

4.   There is no necessary connection between low income households, physical deterioration and social problems.   But in some situations where policies have resulted in high concentrations of low income households there does seem to have been an increase in the problems being discussed.

        Despite the growing concern, governments and social housing organisations are only just beginning to discover the magnitude of the problems which will face them in the years to come.   A great variety of innovative responses is now occurring.   There is as yet insufficient experience of the success or failure of these responses to be able to draw any general conclusions about their value; but, apart from physical strategies - such as the demolition or major improvement of units and the provision of private open space - there have also been attempts, as in Britain, to change the social composition of these areas.   On the whole such efforts are less advanced in the rest of Europe than in Britain (and in the United States), although there is a major effort taking place in France to deal with the problems of some 'grands ensembles' with particularly serious difficulties (Figeat, 1983).

HOUSING MANAGEMENT AND TENANT PARTICIPATION

The problems of the management of social rented housing have already been mentioned in the context of the severe deterioration of certain estates. But dissatisfaction with management is much more widespread. In part this is due to the effects of expediture cutbacks and new practices in reducing service quality; the deleterious effects of some of these supposed savings have already been noted. But often there has also been a rather remote and authoritarian management style. Interestingly, there seems at least as much evidence of this in the purportedly less bureaucratic housing associations and co-operatives which manage most social housing in Europe as in the local authority stock in Britain. The growth in the popularity of owner occupation, where there is greater autonomy, may have contributed to the desire of those who remain in social housing to change its management. Such management may in turn have contributed to the propensity of those who can afford to do so to leave social housing in order to buy or not to enter it in the first place (although the economic motive is likely to have been the most significant single factor in tenure choice).

One response has been to suggest that the larger holdings of social housing should be broken up and/or that management should be decentralised. In West Germany a proposal has been made to hand over housing association properties to smaller, locally based co-operatives, with the creation of regionally based associations to build and rehabilitate units but not manage them. In Denmark the government has recently announced that it intends to pursue very similar policies. In other countries there seems to be a movement towards decentralised forms of management within the existing institutional framework. In Britain, as discussed in chapter 7, there has been much interest in management decentralisation, in connection with efforts to 'turn round' the type of housing estates discussed in the previous section. (These schemes have been influenced by the experiments which have occurred in public housing in the United States.) The new French initiative mentioned above also encompasses attempts to increase tenant participation. But there has been a more general development of tenant consultation and involvement in management. In some cases this goes considerably further than what has occurred in Britain following the Housing Act, 1980. Thus, in the Netherlands, legislation passed in 1977 gave tenants new rights concerning maintenance, rent determination and renovation. Rather similar rights had earlier become available in Denmark. On the whole, though, these rights are basically rights to be consulted and, as in Britain, they fall far short of effective tenant participation in management decisions and policies, or even of any effective means of objecting to decisions when they are put into practice.

In so far as full tenant management is concerned, it is still the case that this has been developed and monitored most extensively in the United States. The lessons to be learnt from these experiments in the management of public housing cannot be discussed here, but the point can be made that there has been no significant growth in the number of estates under this form of management for some years, that it only appears to be a success if certain pre-existing conditions are met (such as a relatively low turnover of tenants and strong incentives for tenants to become involved), and that it cannot successfully be imposed 'top down' (see Rigby, 1982). It seems likely that the conditions which make for success are only likely to be met in a minority of cases; most tenants appear to want improvements in the sensitivity and efficiency of existing management and greater freedom from petty restrictions rather than a transfer to them of total responsibility.

PROSPECTS AND PROBLEMS

Given the current economic situation, whatever the immediate signs of a recovery from the extremely depressed state of the early 1980s, the medium to long-term prospects for the housing sector in Europe are not very bright. This is even more so in the case of social housing. While, at least in the economically more advanced countries of northern Europe, it is arguable that the improvement in housing standards and in the demographic climate in the last decades means that housing problems are less acute than in the past, serious difficulties and dilemmas remain.

The broadest issue concerns the current direction of overall housing policies. With few exceptions there has been a growth of policies which focus on the promotion of owner occupation, and a relative downgrading of political concern for, and support given to, social housing. The immunity, so far at least, of owner occupier subsidies from the cuts which have been imposed on the social sector reflects this situation. But there may be a growing disjunction between the general direction of housing policies and housing market developments which governments will be forced to recognise. The expansion of owner occupation relied heavily on the conditions of full employment and real income growth of the 1960s and 1970s. The first no longer exists, and the second is much less certain and is perhaps restricted to a decreasing proportion of the population. In short, it is not only in the social sector but in the private sector too that there is growing problem of affordability, especially while real interest rates remain high.

In this situation there are a number of possible responses. For example, there could well be a drop in the rate of household formation as young people delay the time at which they cease to live with their parents. There will also be pressure on governments to increase the subsidisation of owner occupation (supported by those who build and finance such housing). Indeed, despite the growth of discussion about the need to cut such subsidies, there have in recent years been several occasions when governments have reacted to the plight of overstretched owner occupiers and the depressed construction industry in just this manner. But there may also be a revival in the demand for rented accommodation and, as the private rented sector is in an even more depressed state than the rest of the private market, this is likely to translate into an increased demand for social rented housing. Already many European countries seem to be experiencing rising waiting lists for this type of accommodation.

In the stronger economies such as West Germany these problems may be resolved or at least considerably alleviated by the resumption of reasonable rates of economic growth, though at the moment this is more of a hope than a certainty. Here the path of continuing expansion of owner occupation and the reduction of social housing to a residual tenure may continue. In countries where the prospects for the expansion of owner occupation seem less revivable the lack of political and/or social acceptability of the social renting alternative may prevent its being adopted. More generally, though, it is the costs of the tenure, in terms of subsidies and higher rents, which are likely to make the return to a substantially expanding social sector problematic - despite any growth in demand. In these cases the 'solution' to many housing needs may in future be found in the growth of 'doubling up' and other means of using space more intensively, the reduction in other housing standards, and increased pressure on household budgets, many of which are already highly stretched.

Beyond this, there are several important matters with which social housing policy will have to grapple. Some of these have been reviewed in this chapter but the issues are often interlinked. Inflation continues to exert upward pressure on subsidies and rents. Yet the degressive subsidies which sought to deal with these problems have, as we have noted, run into difficulties in the current economic situation. In so far as the promotion of owner occupation has contributed to a narrowing of the income distribution of those in social housing, these difficulties have been added to because the scope for changing the balance between the proportion of housing costs that is met by government and by households has been reduced. Moreover, policies which aim to restrict new construction to that which is necessary for those in the greatest need (that is largely those on low incomes) mean that governments are involved in large subsidy commitments for every unit produced. In many cases this problem may well be resolved by further restrictions in the output of new units. In the Netherlands, for example, this is explicitly recognised at present.

These difficulties connect with a further problem area. This is the question of the confinement of social housing to a 'welfare' role. For various reasons, some more securely grounded than others, many governments and non-profit organisations have had a policy of trying to maintain the income mix in social housing because of a belief that large low income housing areas would be more likely to generate the sort of physical and social problems which have been referred to earlier. Yet these social considerations are in conflict with the consequences of economising on subsidies via the withdrawal of general assistance and its replacement by income linked allowances. The point is illustrated by recent developments in France. In 1977 the government decided to raise rents in the social sector, expand housing allowances for those that needed them, and economise on construction subsidies (for a brief account of these reforms see Pearsall, 1984). At the same time, the government continued to express concern about the growth of areas of social housing which were exclusively occupied by low income groups, particularly where these were accompanied by the deterioration of the stock and the growth of social tensions. Yet, in so far as higher rents may encourage tenants to move out and become owner occupiers they may reduce income mix. So the financial and social objectives are in conflict.

There are other dilemmas too. Thus the ability to afford the costs of the rehabilitation of social housing projects, which is now such a central issue in many countries, without an escalating subsidy bill is reduced if there is a decline in the aggregate purchasing power of the tenants living in such areas. In general, while it would be a gross exaggeration to claim that the conditions which led to the financial and physical crisis of much of the public housing stock in large American cities in the last decades exist in European cities, the combination of factors which led to this result (and the heavy costs of responding to it) are not irrelevant for the consideration of future policy directions.

A further set of issues concerns the changing nature of the relations and responsibilities of those involved in social housing provision. In Britain the system of housing planning introduced in the late 1970s has not resulted in the more effective distribution of subsidies and the more sensitive response to local housing needs which were promised. As many observers at the time of the reforms noted, including the present author, these changes could simply be a device for increasing the degree of strategic control that central government has over local housing expenditure, and for delegating still further the responsibility for trying to repond to local needs to local bodies without providing them with the resources to respond adequately (Harloe, 1978b). And so it has turned out to be. This trend towards housing 'planning' has also occurred elsewhere (for example in Sweden, the Netherlands and Italy). But the separation of responsibility for meeting housing needs from control over the resources necessary to achieve housing policies is, in an era of austerity, a somewhat ominous trend. Much the same point can be made concerning the eagerness with which some central and local government agencies are taking up the question of the decentralisation of responsibility for housing services at the local level. The various experiments in tenant management and more locally based housing organisations are, on the one hand, a response to the remoteness and inefficiency of more centralised management. On the other hand, they may involve a similar separation of strategic financial powers and of housing responsibilities to that occurring at the central/local interface. Responsibility without resources is likely to be a false freedom.

Few of these dilemmas and problems are being faced up to, or even fully recognised, in British policy making. There is little evidence that greater progress has been made with them in other European countries, although it must be stressed that there is still a great deal of cross national variation. In fact the current circumstances of social housing are in important respects the product of the general directions taken by housing policies and markets in most European countries in the past 20 or so years. A key factor is the increasing imbalance in the distribution of subsidies between tenures. In addition, inflation has greatly increased the desirability of buying rather than renting, and there is also the more diffuse but nevertheless real impact of the loss of political support for social rented housing and the reduction in its perceived desirability as a housing solution among large sections of the population.

In short, the current problems of European social housing are not wholly or even mainly resolvable by reforms which accept as fixed the position of the other main tenures and the more general context within which housing markets and policies operate (for further discussion see Ball, 1982, 1983; Harloe, 1982). Without some far reaching changes it seems highly likely that these problems will persist and intensify. But it is not possible, in Britain or elsewhere, to be optimistic about the prospects for such changes occurring, whatever may be the political persuasions of the governments concerned.

Chapter Nine

THE NEW FACE OF PUBLIC HOUSING

David Clapham

There is now a great deal of evidence to confirm
that public rented housing in Britain has for some years been
undergoing substantial change, a trend which has been
characterised as 'residualisation' by some commentators.
There is wide agreement on the nature of these changes,
although some argument continues about their extent and
underlying causes. But there is no doubt that central
government, through the right-to-buy legislation and the
manipulation of housing financial controls and subsidies, has
ensured that the public sector stock is declining in both
numerical terms and physical condition. The social
composition of the sector is changing, with the proportion of
lower income households increasing and a growing social
polarisation between it and owner occupation.
Attempts to launch political campaigns against
policies which underlie these changes have not proved to be
successful; witness the fate of successive proposals
concerning income tax relief on mortgage interest. It is
unlikely that any alternative government to the present
Conservative administration will be able radically to alter
these policies and reverse, or even do much to stem, the
decline of public housing. The popularity of the right to
buy, concern about the management practices of local
authorities and the changing subsidy structure have ensured
that the perceived balance of advantage between the tenures
has shifted further towards owner occupation, and have put
advocates of public housing on the defensive. This has led
to rethinking about the desirable form and role of public
rental housing, and has led to a wealth of alternative
policies. However, the policy prescriptions are as varied
as the people putting them forward and it is difficult to
make much sense of the tangled web of proposals. The
primary focus has been on the two areas of subsidies and
management policies. There have been numerous attempts to
design a subsidy system which is tenure neutral and channels
help to those most in need (Gray, Hepworth and Odling-Smee,
1978; Ermisch, 1984), but no consensus has emerged as to the

most desirable scheme to pursue; there is widespread
scepticism about the ability of any future government to
carry through significant reforms, which would undoubtedly
threaten the interests of many owner occupiers. The
proposals concerning local authority management are just as
varied, as chapter 7 showed, and again no consensus has
emerged even about the general direction which change should
take.

All too rarely are financial and management issues
combined and an attempt made to put forward a coherent view
of the role of public rented housing. One of the few
examples of this is Webster's notion of a 'social market' in
housing (Webster, 1981) where local housing authorities are
seen as entrepreneurs reacting to demand rather than need - a
change of approach which is dependent on, and coupled with,
both a tenure neutral housing finance system and reforms to
housing management practices. Attempts such as this to
present a coherent view of a future role for public sector
housing are rare. More usually, various policy proposals
are viewed rather like constituents of a smorgasbord from
which any number and combination of elements can be chosen,
regardless of whether they are contradictory or together add
up to a coherent package.

Nevertheless, there are two major themes which
underlie many of the proposals. The first is a movement
away from the concept of public rented housing being
primarily geared to those in housing need, however that is
defined. There are repeated references to catering for
those who wish to rent irrespective of need, and to
responding to demand rather than need. The slogan 'right to
rent', coined by the Labour Housing Group, sums up an
approach which stresses the desirability of allowing those
who wish to rent from a local authority to be able to do so
whether or not they are in housing need as defined by the
local authority. The sector is, therefore, urged to meet
aspirations rather than merely need, and be more responsive
to the wishes of both existing and prospective tenants.
Paternalism in management does not fit with this approach,
and the emphasis is on a contractual management relationship,
with local authorities clearly separating their housing from
their social service functions.

The second major theme is that of making the sector
more locally based and increasing the control which tenants
can exert. This means that the emphasis should be on the
decentralisation of many housing functions to a local level,
and the devolution of power to tenants through increased
participation in management decisions or the creation of
tenant management co-operatives. It is recognised that
council tenants have much less control over their housing
situation than owner occupiers, and for many households this
is an important factor in choosing between the two tenures.

These two themes, both of which are present, for example, in current Labour Party thinking, can be seen to be complementary to some extent, although they may be contradictory and they conceal many problems of detail. To take the example of allocation policies, the two themes both stress a movement away from allocation according to need which, although it has had varied interpretations and may be difficult to recognise in practice, has been the traditional rationale behind local authority lettings procedures. Nevertheless, the first approach stresses more freedom of choice for prospective tenants and a dismantling of traditional rationing processes in order to move towards a system of public housing on demand. It is difficult, however, to see how this could be achieved in the current situation where demand for many council dwellings far outstrips supply, unless rent levels were manipulated by introducing a form of market pricing to equilibrate supply and demand. The second emphasis on a locally-based service would involve devolving power over allocations to local tenants' groups, possibly with the local authority retaining nomination rights over a proportion of lettings. This suggestion has been criticised because of the bias which it is supposed tenants would have against, for example, ethnic minorities or so-called problem families.

No consensus has emerged about which of these routes should be taken and how either of them could be put into practice successfully. Much more thought, debate and experience are needed before a coherent and practicable alternative view of the future role of the public sector can be put forward. However, some of this experience is already being gained by a substantial number of councils which, instead of waiting for a change in central government policy, have responded to recent constraints and pressures on public housing by pursuing local initiatives, many of which are related to the second theme of localising the public housing system. Some of these initiatives are supported by central government but others are not. The result is a set of initiatives which, although they bear little resemblance to each other, together could change the nature of public sector housing; it is to these we should look, rather than to changes in government policy on housing finance, in attempting to understand the form the public sector may take in the foreseeable future. The four major initiatives are privatisation, decentralisation, community ownership and management co-operatives.

PRIVATISATION

The most widely applied initiative is privatisation of public sector blocks of flats or even whole estates. Forrest notes this initiative in chapter 5 and argues that it is a logical extension of the council house sales programme. There are limits to individual sales, both in terms of the availability of properties of a type and location which households want to buy and the number of households which, at least in the short term, are able to buy; therefore, if the momentum of sales into owner occupation is to be continued, emphasis will also have to be given to 'mass privatisation'. However, privatisation is not only motivated by the desire to promote home ownership by central government and local authorities, as Forrest perhaps implies; it may also be seen by the latter as a way out of the problems experienced by the public sector and in particular as the only practicable means of obtaining the renovation of property given limits on capital spending. Privatisation is as much a response to constraints operating on local authorities as any commitment by them to home ownership.

Mass privatisation can take a number of forms, one of which is the sale of council housing to a private developer for renovation and resale into owner occupation. Unless a difficult-to-let area has already become empty, this process involves moving existing tenants, and the power of local authorities compulsorily to rehouse those with secure status was in doubt. But the Housing and Planning Bill which will be passed during 1986 specifically gives them such a power where property is being sold for renovation. A different form of privatisation is where tenanted housing is sold; so far this has only occurred or been proposed in the case of sales to co-operatives or trusts of various types. In some examples, the properties remain wholly rented (subject to individual households' right to buy), and initiatives of this kind are dealt with later under community ownership. But other initiatives involve renovation and resale, and possibly also new building, for owner occupation, as well as continued renting; here the involvement of outside institutions such as building societies may drastically restrict the degree of resident control. Privatisation schemes, especially sales to developers for renovation and resale, are being actively promoted by the Urban Housing Renewal Unit, which was set up within the Department of the Environment in 1985 to advise local authorities and private institutions on ways of dealing with run down areas.

Privatisation initiatives of the more straightforward kind are widespread; for example Liverpool and Salford have sold blocks of flats to private developers and Wandsworth whole estates. In Edinburgh the council sold half of the West Pilton estate (over 700 properties) to a private developer for refurbishment and resale for owner occupation. The remainder of the estate is to be retained and improved by the council, which argued that it could not afford to improve whole estates out of its capital allocation (Hague, 1985). Spencerbeck Estate, in Langbaurgh on Teeside, is being sold on the grounds that the council lacks the resources to maintain the (apparently pleasant and popular) houses.

The best-known example of the privatisation of tenanted estates is Cantril Farm, or Stockbridge Village as it is now called, in Knowsley near Liverpool which is an overspill and slum clearance estate built in the late 1960s and early 1970s. The estate was planned to house some 14,000 people, although the actual population never rose above 11,000. It consisted of a mixture of houses, multi-storey blocks and four-storey maisonette blocks, and the layout was poor with vast areas of badly-maintained open space. Before the Stockbridge Village Trust was formed to buy the properties and revitalise the area, Cantril Farm exhibited in a heightened form most of the problems which have afflicted some public housing. Unemployment in the area was very high, the unpopular maisonette blocks were generally let to homeless families who had no other choice, vacancies were high as were rent arrears, only eight properties had been purchased under the right-to-buy legislation, and the environment and the dwellings themselves were in a poor state. The council did not have the resources to revitalise the area and, therefore, sold the estate to a trust made up of several financial institutions as well as two representatives from the local area. The trust has carried out a mixture of physical and social changes. It is planned to demolish unpopular maisonette blocks, refurbish the multi-storey blocks and replan the street layout. New housing is to be built on vacant land by a housing association formed for this purpose. The social changes have involved moving out many of the most disadvantaged tenants and encouraging more affluent households from elsewhere to move into newly-built or refurbished property, much of which is to be sold for owner occupation. It is hoped that half the properties will eventually be owner occupied and half rented, either from a housing association or from the trust itself.

The financial objectives for pursuing a privatisation strategy generally appear to be particularly important: local authorities are faced with deteriorating neighbourhoods, while financial controls prevent them from carrying out the necessary physical improvements. Privatisation is an effective way of getting the improvements done - the physical transformation of Stockbridge Village is impressive - but the financial benefits to the local authority are rather nebulous. The property is usually sold to the developer at a relatively low price and the local authority is only allowed, through an expanded capital allocation, to spend a proportion of the receipts in any one year. Nevertheless, in some cases this can constitute a substantial sum. Of course, the short-term financial advantages may not be reflected in the longer term where gains or losses are more difficult to predict because of the many imponderables which have to be taken into account. But the evidence points to substantial losses, both to the individual local authority as rents would have outstripped falling real debt charges, and, at least where the houses become owner occupied, to the public purse in general, as income tax. relief is made available to successive purchasers. It is not clear whether the private sector financing institutions find their financial returns entirely satisfactory, although this may not be a problem for them as the loans are often guaranteed by the local authority, but there is some evidence that developers have not always made the profits they hoped for when the properties were sold into owner occupation. However, the availability of urban development grants from central government may encourage many developers to involve themselves in such schemes. These grants can be very large; for example £800,000 when the Spencerbeck estate was sold to Barratts. The problems are much greater when, as in Stockbridge Village, some of the properties continue to be rented and, because they are no longer in the public sector, fall under the 'fair rent' procedure. In Stockbridge this resulted in a rental level which did not give the trust the income it required and called into question the viability of the project. These problems have added to pressures on the government to remove rent controls, and have led to calls for the provision of revenue subsidy to private developers. Because of the doubts about the financial return, at this stage it is difficult to assess whether the interest of private sector institutions in public housing areas will be sustained in the long term; much will depend on future government policy.

But, if the financial advantages of privatisation are nebulous (except, almost certainly, to individual purchasers), the social advantages are perhaps even more so. Where all the tenants are moved out of the property and rehoused by the local authority, and the improved properties are sold to incoming owner occupiers, the change in social status and often household structure is pronounced, disadvantaged families with children being replaced by more affluent childless couples. In contrast, in schemes such as Stockbridge Village where a rental element will continue to exist and at West Pilton where only part of the estate was sold, the changes are likely to lead to a more balanced community with a break-up of the concentration of deprived households and a reduction in child density. But the households moved from the areas still have to be housed in the public sector and care has to be exercised to prevent similar concentrations of disadvantaged families elsewhere. Whilst privatisation schemes may change the social structure of the areas in which they are tried, they could have detrimental effects in other areas and they do nothing to inhibit the socio-economic polarisation of the two major tenures or to reverse the overall decline in the numbers of properties available for rent.

Although some of the original residents of these areas benefit from the changes, many do not and there have been fierce battles fought by tenants in both Cantril Farm and West Pilton against the privatisation proposals. Consultation was minimal and in Cantril Farm tenants effectively had a choice of privatisation or no action to improve conditions. It is not surprising, given the existing conditions, that many opted for privatisation although deep divisions existed. In general, residents have had little or no control over the renewal process, and the advantage of greater control over housing through owner occupation has gone largely to outsiders. Tenants of the Stockbridge Village Trust have little more control over their housing conditions than when they were tenants of the council. They have been told that their two representatives do not have to face re-election. The whole process is often imposed on local communities from outside, giving them little influence over their own future.

Privatisation may offer a solution to the problems of some areas which provides a mechanism whereby physical improvements can be undertaken without drawing on limited public sector funding. However, there are other ways of using private finance to renovate public housing whilst giving tenants more say over the process, as the example of community ownership in Glasgow, discussed in detail later, shows.

DECENTRALISATION

There appears to be a fairly general trend towards the decentralisation of local authority services, though the trend is strongest and most developed in public housing where it is being applied to both management and maintenance functions. Many local housing authorities, particularly rural ones, have operated on a decentralised basis for many years, but others are now moving at varying speeds in this direction.

Decentralisation is a very general term which hides a great variety of specific objectives and practices. The objectives can be divided into the managerial and political. Managerial objectives are concerned with the efficiency and effectiveness of management and maintenance services, in providing a better and more accessible service to tenants and maintaining the stock in good condition. They may also be concerned with effective co-ordination between services, for example between housing management and social services departments, to provide a more comprehensive and co-ordinated service to residents. The political objectives are more far-reaching; they range from providing a 'friendlier' service to tenants to altering fundamentally the relationship between the local authority and residents and, therefore, between public landlord and tenant. The political objectives represent the major difference between recent decentralisation initiatives and those pursued in the 1970s (see, for example, Hambleton, 1978) which were mainly concerned with managerial objectives. The use of decentralisation for political objectives can be related to changes in the Labour Party and in the position of local government relative to central government. Within the Labour Party there is an increasing willingness to use local government as a campaigning vehicle which is partly related to a change in perspective concerning the role of the 'local state'. Cockburn (1977) argued against community development and local action, which she believed led to the incorporation of the working class in the apparatus of the local state. This view, which was shared by many local councillors, has been replaced by a belief that local action, through mechanisms such as decentralisation, is the way to recover the lost sense of 'community' among the working class (Seabrook, 1984), and to reconnect an increasingly middle class Labour Party with its working class roots. At the same time, Labour-controlled local authorities have come under increasing pressure from a Conservative government which has over-ridden local mandates. 'Building from the bottom' (Blunkett and Green, 1983) is seen as a way of re-establishing these mandates by mobilising local support against central government.

Of course, the implicit assumption behind this approach is that feelings and attitudes in local areas will correspond with the views and policy of the Labour Party. This is obviously not always the case and has led to a reluctance on the part of some local authorities to devolve power over decentralised administrative units to residents in areas of strong Conservative Party support. Decentralisation of policy-making is sometimes considered to be only appropriate as long as residents toe the party line. The mixture of managerial and political objectives makes decentralisation a very complex phenomenon which is difficult to pin down and almost impossible to evaluate. This complexity is further enhanced by the variations in the mechanisms by which decentralisation is to be achieved. Some local authorities, such as Islington and Hackney, have attempted what has been called the 'big bang' approach, that is decentralising a wide range of services across the whole of the borough. For example, Islington plans to decentralise housing management, social services, planning, environmental health, street cleansing and welfare rights to 24 neighbourhood offices throughout the borough.

Many local authorities have found that implementation of the 'big bang' approach has not proved to be an easy task. The costs of building neighbourhood offices have been high and finding sites for them in some areas has been difficult. Local authority staff have not always welcomed the initiative and in some cases have blocked it completely. In Islington a substantial regrading of jobs, carried out to overcome union objections, has increased the salary bill, leading to estimates of the cost of decentralisation of around £3 million per annum.

These difficulties have led to many authorities rejecting the 'big bang' approach and instead adopting a more incremental and cautious one, either by decentralising only one or possibly two departments, by decentralising only to certain areas, or by a gradual reduction in scale of existing operations. In most of these approaches the housing service has been the focus of decentralisation, partly because it is often already decentralised to some degree and partly because the advantages of a decentralised housing service have been clearly demonstrated by, for example, the Priority Estates Project (PEP) initiatives which have been described in chapter 7. There are some problems with the evaluation which has been undertaken of the PEP schemes in that it has been largely subjective and carried out by members of the schemes themselves; but it has shown to many people's satisfaction that intensive local management, allied with a locally organised repairs service and a locally administered allocation policy, can bring a variety of benefits. In the short term at least it can improve the efficiency and cost effectiveness of service delivery and lead to a better service to tenants, an improvement in the social and physical environment of an area and higher levels of tenant satisfaction. Housing is one service where the managerial objectives may correspond with the political ones, whereas in other services they may well be in conflict.

Decentralisation has taken many different forms in practice. Initiatives vary in the scale of decentralised units, the functions decentralised, the degree of autonomy which the decentralised unit has vis-a-vis the centre, and the degree of control exercised by residents and local politicians over the policies and practices of the decentralised unit. The last dimension is particularly important if decentralisation is to achieve its political objectives as well as its managerial ones. In the decentralised housing system in Walsall there is no mechanism for residents to influence local offices, and other local authorities such as Islington have yet to come to terms with the dilemmas involved. How are local committees to be constructed? Should they consist of local councillors or political nominees, representatives of local organisations, elected by local residents or some mixture of these? What happens when the wishes of the local community differ from the political stance of the council? These are issues which have proved difficult for local authorities to resolve and, therefore, they have tended to be pushed to one side. If they are not confronted, however, it seems unlikely that the political objective of fundamentally altering the relationship between local government and residents is achievable by merely providing the same service administered locally.

The case for reducing the scale of the housing management and maintenance service appears to be justified on managerial grounds, although much more research needs to be done before this can be stated unequivocally. As far as political objectives are concerned, more thought requires to be given to problems involved in achieving them, and it may be that other mechanisms such as community ownership may be a more effective strategy. However, the impact of a more efficient and responsive management service on the current position of public housing could be substantial, and it could help to reverse the physical and social deterioration in many estates which reinforce the view of the sector as a tenure of last resort. It could also result in a more diverse sector, with management policies and the extent and direction of tenants' influence varying considerably according to local conditions and to the wishes, aspirations and capacities of local residents.

The major drawback with decentralisation as a strategy for public housing is that it does not in itself lead to any more financial resources being made available for physical improvements to the dwellings. Decentralisation is, therefore, only satisfactory in areas of unsound housing if it is coupled with an injection of capital expenditure; it should not be seen as an alternative to capital investment. Community ownership, however, offers a way of both decentralising the housing service and injecting capital funding at the same time.

COMMUNITY OWNERSHIP

Community ownership is the name given to proposals drawn up in Glasgow which combine elements of both of the previous approaches. It involves transferring small areas of public housing to co-operatives which will purchase the properties from the council. Residents will collectively own the housing although individual members will not be able to sell their interest in a co-operative. Thus, when a resident leaves, the dwelling reverts to the co-operative which can allocate it again. The residents will control management and maintenance policy, although the council will retain some control over allocations by reserving nomination rights on a proportion of lettings. Three pilot schemes were proposed in 1985, which vary in size from 90 to 360 dwellings. Two of the estates are made up of post-war tenemental properties whereas the other is an inter-war cottage estate. The impetus for setting up the schemes came from the need to upgrade the properties and the inadequacy of public sector capital allocations available to the local authority to finance improvements. However, lessons had

153

been learnt from previous privatisation initiatives such as Stockbridge Village, and there was a determination to ensure that the schemes would be for the benefit of local residents, who would be able to exert as much control as possible over their own housing circumstances, albeit within the constraints of the overall social priorities laid down by the council, exemplified by its powers over the allocation of dwellings.

Under the original proposals which were not accepted by the Secretary of State for Scotland, loans were to have been provided by private financial institutions, that is building societies or banks. The co-operatives would then have improved the properties with the aid of improvement grants. These financial arrangements involved transferring the properties to the co-operatives at a price which would ensure that initial rents would not have to rise above existing levels in order to meet the outgoings. Thus properties would, in some cases, have been transferred at below market price and, in one case, it was proposed to dispose of them at a price which was below the level of the outstanding debt. This is no more than is often done when selling properties to private developers, but the capital receipts to the local authority, some of which could be spent on the remaining public sector stock, would not have been great. At the same time, where a cost rent co-operative of this kind does go ahead, residents can look forward to falling real rents; this is because debt service and repayment are the largest element in outgoings but, rather like an owner occupier's mortgage, they will diminish in real terms assuming the existence of inflation. There may, therefore, be implications for the allocation of vacant houses if rents become substantially lower than those in the public sector. Although there is no evidence that residents when given responsibility for allocation do not base their decisions on housing need, Glasgow opted for a mixed system with the council reserving nomination rights over a proportion of the lettings.

The Secretary of State for Scotland did not approve the financial arrangements proposed by Glasgow District Council and he required that the co-operatives should be registered with the Housing Corporation. This means that they will receive Housing Association Grant (and are thus not dependent on private sector financing) but that rents will be determined under the fair rent procedure. The arrangement is clearly financially less attractive to tenants than the original proposal but the groups of tenants concerned decided to go ahead. The council is examining how cost rent co-operatives could be set up in the future in a way which is acceptable to the government.

The mechanism finally adopted in Glasgow, the co-operative, was the same as that chosen by Liverpool City Council in its short-lived attempts to give residents more control over the rehabilitation of their properties. It is also similar to the proposals put forward by the Centre for Policy Studies for housing management trusts, which would be controlled by trustees made up of local residents and nominees from financial institutions and local authorities (Henney, 1985). A community trust is being set up in Thamesmead, formerly a GLC estate, with backing from both central government and local tenants. Tenants were balloted in October 1985 and were asked to choose between the trust and an alternative proposal put forward by the London Borough of Greenwich for the property to be taken over by the council. Tenants voted to set up the trust which will be controlled by elected local residents and which will buy the 6,000 properties from the London Residuary Body (which took them over from the GLC when it was abolished). Finance will be provided from private financial institutions.

Although the Liverpool initiative was ended by the incoming Labour administration in 1982, and the Glasgow schemes are only pilot projects, the degree of interest shown by other local authorities and, perhaps more importantly, by tenants suggests that given sufficient support there is considerable potential for these developments. In the latter years of the Liverpool initiative more potential co-operatives were coming forward than could be funded and Glasgow has a waiting list of about a dozen groups of tenants anxious to take over their houses.

MANAGEMENT CO-OPERATIVES

The nature of management co-operatives was examined with some examples in chapter 7. This is one of the most longstanding initiatives in public housing; some co-operatives having been in existence since the mid-1970s. There is, therefore, considerable experience in setting up and running them, although this has not been brought together in a systematic way which would allow firm conclusions to be drawn about their effectiveness. However, it appears that the experience has, in general, been satisfactory from the point of view both of residents, who have been more involved in the management of their estates and have received a better service as a result, and of local housing authorities which have seen the effort involved in setting up the co-operatives repaid by the tenants taking responsibility for day-to-day management. It is difficult to reconcile this apparent success with the fact that only a few management co-operatives exist outside London and Glasgow, and that very few have been set up since about 1983. The idea has obviously not been accepted as widely as some of its advocates envisaged. This may be due to the attitude of local housing authorities - there is no doubt that many have not encouraged or have sometimes even actively discouraged their formation - but even in Glasgow, where there are

already eight co-operatives in existence and the local
authority actively encourages their formation, progress has
been slow.

There are obviously constraints on the ability and
willingness of residents to spend time and effort on forming
and running a co-operative. Residents in management
co-operatives are often asked to administer management and
maintenance services as well as control them with little
professional help. This contrasts with the situation of
many co-operatives in the housing association sector which
can call on the specialised services of a secondary
co-operative that will administer services whilst leaving
residents in control of major decisions.

The deterioration of the public sector stock has
also played an important part, in that residents have been
unwilling to take responsibility for the maintenance of stock
which is in a bad condition or in need of improvement. The
control which residents can exert over the physical condition
of the stock is largely limited to what can be done through a
jobbing repair service, and even the money which can be spent
on this has to be negotiated with the local authority.
Management co-operatives can thus spend substantial amounts
of money patching up property which needs modernisation by,
for example, repeatedly repairing windows which really should
be replaced. In these circumstances community ownership is
a more attractive proposition for both residents and local
authorities. However, the management co-operative remains
an important option for the public sector which can be of
value in many circumstances.

The introduction of these initiatives -
privatisation, decentralisation, community ownership and
management co-operatives - suggests that the nature of public
sector housing is changing in response to
'residualisation'. Three features of these changes common
to most of the initiatives are particularly important. These
are the changing relationship between the public and private
sectors, the reduction in scale of housing management and the
increasing role of residents, which are now considered in
turn.

PUBLIC-PRIVATE SECTOR INTERRELATIONSHIPS

These initiatives show that private institutions
are beginning to play an increasing role in the public
sector. The distinction between the public and private
sectors has never been clear cut, in that public sector
institutions have actively involved themselves in the
promotion of owner occupation in many different ways. Indeed,
both Murie and Forrest, in chapters 2 and 5 respectively,
suggest, perhaps with tongue in cheek, that owner occupation
should be viewed as the real public sector. Private sector
institutions, on the other hand, have always been involved in

the provision of public housing by, for example, providing land, lending capital finance and undertaking most of the actual building. However, their involvement is becoming more direct. In the Stockbridge Village Trust private sector institutions own and manage the housing as well as providing the finance for its renovation. In the Glasgow community ownership proposals in their original form the residents themselves would have owned and managed the properties using finance made available by private sector institutions.

It is not yet clear whether this involvement is a short-lived public relations exercise by banks, building societies and developers or whether it represents a more permanent change. The involvement of building societies may be an indication that they are beginning to plan for the end of the expansion of owner occupation by supporting schemes such as community ownership and the Stockbridge Village Trust. The position of private developers is more difficult to judge, and it remains to be seen whether the financial returns are sufficient to retain their interest in taking over property from the public sector. The willingness of local authorities to continue with these initiatives is also subject to some uncertainty. There is no doubt that many local authorities have been forced to involve themselves with private sector institutions solely because of the constraints, particularly financial, operating on them. If these financial constraints were eased by central government, there is little doubt that few local authorities would then take this course, and that most would finance improvements from public funds and retain ownership. It is clear that the major motivation for tenants in Glasgow to join the community ownership scheme was to get their homes repaired and modernised, and that taking over ownership was a secondary consideration. If the council had offered to carry out the work themselves and retain ownership, the tenants would most likely have been satisfied.

Although many local authorities have taken this general route, the particular form of the partnership has varied considerably. Stockbridge Village Trust, for example, is a far cry from the community ownership proposals. This largely reflects the innovative nature of the schemes and the lack of a tried and tested solution. However, it may also reflect different local conditions and objectives. It will be interesting to see whether the present diversity is reflected in future schemes or whether existing initiatives will be copied.

REDUCTION IN SCALE OF HOUSING MANAGEMENT

Another common thread running through the initiatives is the reduction in scale of housing management. Decentralisation and the Priority Estates

157

Project are the most obvious examples of this, but the community ownership schemes all consist of no more than 360 dwellings, and in Stockbridge Village the number of rented properties is many fewer than was managed from the previous area office which was not even situated on the estate. This reduction in scale is partly a matter of policy but it also reflects the fact that the innovations have sometimes stemmed from the need to deal with the concentration of the worst problems in fairly small areas, which become unmanageable using traditional means.

The reduction in scale is designed to achieve more effective management in terms of services which can be provided more efficiently in the narrow economic sense, as well as being more in tune with the needs and demands of local residents. The move towards centralisation of housing management and maintenance which was widespread in the 1960s and 1970s largely occurred because it was thought that economies of scale could be achieved. These are now thought by many local authorities and tenants' organisations to be illusory but this judgement has not been backed up by much evidence. There do appear to be some economies and evidence of a better service to tenants to be derived from reducing the scale of repair services, but the gathering of evidence about other functions has been hampered by difficulties in defining what constitutes good housing management and how the effectiveness of management can be measured. This lack of substantive evidence can be dangerous, in that it leaves policy open to whims of fashion. It is currently fashionable to reduce the scale of housing management, but unless there is evidence of an improvement in the management service, or a reduction of costs in achieving the same level of service, fashion could easily change again.

There has been some opposition to the reduction in scale of housing management, chiefly from trade unions concerned about job prospects and career structures. A decentralised service could lead to a change in the career structure in housing management with fewer high level jobs. It could also lead to a change in the nature of jobs, as housing managers come more into contact with, and become more accountable to, tenants. There is no doubt that some housing staff do not relish this situation, as was shown by the determination of trade unions in Glasgow to keep defensive barriers and grilles in local offices as protection from tenants. However, decentralisation has often been associated with privatisation or with a much greater involvement of tenants as in community ownership, situations where it may be thought that the jobs of existing local authority employees are in any case threatened.

INCREASING THE ROLE OF RESIDENTS

An increased role for residents is a feature of some of the initiatives but not others. Where dwellings become owner occupied, individuals obviously gain more control over their housing situation. In the Glasgow community ownership proposals residents will communally own the properties, controlling management and most other functions, subject to Housing Corporation scrutiny. The position in Stockbridge Village is different in that the trust which manages the rented properties is made up of representatives of the financing bodies and has only two representatives from the local community. This arrangement ensures that residents have some say in their future, but they do not have control. The position of residents in decentralised systems such as Islington's is more difficult to assess, and seems to differ both between and within local authorities. In no case have residents been given complete control over the operations of local offices, and often, indeed, no formal mechanism has been set up through which residents can exert influence. The assumption sometimes seems to be that the creation of decentralised units in themselves will fundamentally change the role of residents, although this seems very unlikely. A similar equivocal stance is adopted in the Priority Estates Project where the degree of resident influence varies between schemes and invariably stops well short of control.

CONCLUSION

It is evident that the new initiatives – privatisation, decentralisation, community ownership and management co-operatives – are very different from each other. The lack of a tried and tested model of private sector involvement, the localised nature of many of the initiatives, and the autonomy given to them to respond to the wishes and needs of local residents mean that variety is inevitable. Of course, the precise nature of public sector housing, in terms of the rights and influence of tenants and of the organisation and style of management, has always varied from local authority to local authority. However, the effect of recent changes has been to increase this variation considerably. Public housing as community ownership, for example, is very different from the traditional view of the sector. Taken together these initiatives may radically alter the nature of public housing although it is not clear exactly in which direction the changes are leading. There is no consensus about the appropriate direction, and different people are pursuing different visions of what the housing system should look like. Nor are these visions confined to the housing sector, but can also be seen to be influencing measures such as privatisation and decentralisation in other social services. However, they appear to be more developed in housing than elsewhere, which is probably because of the unique nature of housing as a commodity and of the organisation of the housing system. As Whitehead (1983) observes, housing is essentially a private good with few externalities. In other words, the benefits and disbenefits of housing largely accrue to the individual owner or user of the property rather than to the community at large. Whitehead, therefore, concludes 'housing is a readily marketable commodity suitable for private provision in a mixed economy' (Whitehead 1983, p. 117). Indeed, the housing system already constitutes much more of a mixed economy with public, private and voluntary organisations all involved in its provision. Also, questioning of the value of professional judgement and pressure for individual control in the use and management of housing are more advanced than in other services. All this means that housing is at the forefront of change.

The initiatives outlined in this chapter may be seen as being consistent with a desire to ensure that housing is primarily a privately owned and marketed commodity, and that wherever possible state provision is replaced by private provision. The sale of council houses, whether individually to sitting tenants or on a larger scale to private developers, obviously fits in with this view. Central government has made no secret of its ambition to increase private sector provision at· the expense of the public sector. However, there is also evidence in recent developments of an alternative vision of the housing system, in terms of the production of a mixed economy rather than a privatised market system. This mixed economy represents a shift in the nature of public involvement, from an emphasis on direct state provision to state regulation of a wide range of non-profit providers such as housing associations, co-operatives and community organisations. This can be seen as a move towards the decentralised and participative system of provision put forward for social services in general by Hadley and Hatch (1981). They advocate a change of emphasis away from the traditional objectives of state provided social services, of uniformity, hierarchial accountability and administrative standardisation, to a system relying on community-based organisations and designed for flexibility, accountability to consumers and deprofessionalisation. Initiatives such as decentralisation and the promotion of ownership and management co-operatives fall into this new style of social service. Indeed, if these initiatives continue to grow it is possible to foresee a situation where it may be necessary to revise the definition of public housing as the role of public institutions changes. Traditionally public housing has been owned and managed by local authorities which have also been largely responsible for strategic planning through the mechanism of housing investment programmes (and housing plans in Scotland) as well as for developing specific housing schemes. The only major role of the private sector in public housing has been in actual building and even here a significant proportion of the work has been carried out by councils themselves through their direct labour organisations. It is possible to foresee a substantially different picture in the next few years if the initiatives discussed here survive and expand. Ownership of public housing may increasingly be vested in local bodies such as trusts and co-operatives with residents themselves playing a larger role than hitherto. Management may be carried out in a variety of ways. In some cases it may be organised by the residents themselves, and in others through a secondary co-operative or a private profit-making management company. Local authorities could find themselves in a situation in which they have to compete to sell their management services to residents.

As developers, local authorities could find themselves working much more closely with private sector institutions such as building societies, banks or private developers as well as with local residents. They may therefore need to develop new areas of expertise and become more entrepreneurial in attitude. It may well be that the local authority setting is the wrong one for this kind of activity and that separate organisations on the lines of the Swedish municipal housing companies will be set up which would be independent from local government and self financing. This would leave local authorities with the major task of housing planning, that is assessing need within their areas and ensuring that the right number, type and size of houses are built in the right place, and also in offsetting housing disadvantage and pursuing social goals. If they were to do this in a devolved system of ownership their existing powers would need to be strengthened substantially.

This is speculation, however, and it is easy to over-emphasise the degree of change which is occurring in public sector housing; as yet only a small minority of tenants has been involved in any of the initiatives. It can alo be argued that the developments are the equivalent of re-arranging the deckchairs on the Titanic, making little or no difference to the overall position of public housing. They can be seen as of slight importance compared with the forces, above all taxation and the system of financial assistance, making for the rapid polarisation of housing tenures and the decline of the public sector. Despite these reservations, however, the new initiatives raise important policy issues and set an agenda for research on and discussion of public housing.

It is perhaps unlikely that all of the initiatives will survive, or at least be significantly extended. Some may prove to be unworkable, to be of little practical

161

relevance or to lead to undesirable consequences. Circumstances facing the public sector may change, altering the objectives of councillors and tenants and thus resulting in a renewed search for fresh initiatives or perhaps a recourse to older solutions. Also, it is most unlikely that one solution will be universally acknowledged as the way forward for public housing. Rather, a range of initiatives will exist, each of which may be seen as appropriate in certain situations and not in others. Which initiatives survive will depend on decisions made by central government, local authorities, housing administrators, members of financial institutions and tenants. It is to be hoped that these decisions are made in the light of practical experience and relevant research, rather than the unproven assertions and whims of fashion which appear to have too often been major factors in the past, as the swing between centralisation and decentralisation of housing management demonstrates.

If the initiatives are to be properly assessed and lessons learnt, much more thought and research must be directed to three major issues. First, more needs to be known about the effectiveness of housing management. Second, the issue of the influence of tenants needs to be addressed. Third, the effects of localising control of public housing on the ability of a local authority to achieve its objectives need to be assessed.

As far as the first area for research is concerned, answers need to be found to fundamental questions such as how housing management can be monitored and assessed and whether the new initiatives make any difference to the standard of management. The Audit Commission (1986) has attempted to measure the effectiveness of housing management in local authorities by using indicators of performance which are compared with costs. This approach has only limited applicability. It may be possible to find indicators of performance in the jobbing repairs service which command universal agreement, such as the length of time taken to do a repair and its cost. But how is the effectiveness of an allocation policy to be defined and measured? Objective indicators have their place but they must be supplemented by subjective assessments. Effective housing management is not just efficient in the narrow cost minimisation sense but it should also meet the needs of tenants as they see them. Tenant views of the service, informed by the performance indicators which are available, are the key to assessing the effectiveness of management. However, the job satisfaction of housing management staff must also be taken into account, not only because people should be considered as producers as well as consumers but because their morale is likely to influence attitudes towards tenants and thus the quality of the service. The views of local councillors are important as well because, although the primary objective of housing management is to serve tenants, local authorities do have responsibilities to people in their areas as a whole which may demand some influence over management policies. For example, there may be a conflict of interest between tenants and would-be tenants in the allocation of properties which can only be resolved through the political process. These four elements, therefore, need to be built into any kind of evaluation of housing management.

Second, different kinds of influence or control which these initiatives allow tenants to take need to be assessed. Even with decentralisation, tenants are left in a bargaining position with housing management staff who can effectively still make all the decisions. The ability of tenants to influence management will be dependent both on their power and on the formal participation structures which are evolved. It remains to be seen whether decentralisation, by making information more readily available to tenants and giving them greater access to decision-makers, will increase their influence over housing management. In community ownership and management co-operatives, residents are given control over some important functions, including management and maintenance. However, this does not necessarily mean that they can exercise effective control over these functions because they may be constrained by a lack of knowledge or time or by the decisions of financial institutions. Again it is important to ascertain whether these constraints are real and to compare experience between the different initiatives.

Third, it is important to know what the effects of localising public housing and devolving control to tenants will be on the ability of local housing authorities to achieve their objectives. Most local authorities, although not all, would consider that they had a general duty to oversee the condition of housing in their areas as well as ensuring that a satisfactory quantity and quality of housing is available. Most authorities would also consider that they had some responsibility for disadvantaged groups in the population such as the mentally and physically handicapped, the elderly and the poor. Local authorities have an obligation to pursue interests which are wider in scope than the needs of one particular housing estate. The question is, therefore, whether councils can achieve these wider social objectives satisfactorily in situations where they do not have full control over the public sector stock. Fears about the loss of local authority power have played an important part in the debate over tenants' control of housing. In particular, concern has often been expressed about giving tenants control over allocation policy because it is thought that they cannot be trusted not to discriminate against 'problem families' or ethnic minorities. This debate has continued without any evidence being produced about what policies tenants who have been given control over

local allocations have pursued.   Some evidence on the
achievement of local authorities in a devolved system may be
gleaned from Norway, where in Oslo the city council converted
most of its stock into co-operatives in the 1950s.   It now
has only some 2,000 properties in its ownership, and it
operates chiefly through the co-operative sector by
nominating tenants and influencing new building.   This has
undoubtedly led to problems and the council now wants to
build public housing under its own control again.   Allowing
for the different context in Norway, evaluation of why these
problems have occurred could provide some guidance as to the
methods of operation which could be adopted by local
authorities in Britain.

        These three issues are important if debate is to be
extended from analysis of the residualisation of public
housing, with which in various ways the contributions to this
book are concerned, to an assessment of the strategies which
are designed to cope with the process.   A considerable body
of research evidence about residualisation and the social
polarisation of tenure and their causes, some of which is
presented in the book, has now been built up.   Although
there may be arguments of detail, there can be little dispute
about the main trends which are continuing to change the
respective roles of the public sector and owner occupation
within the British housing system.   The concern of
politicians, tenants' organisations and housing policy
analysts needs to be extended to what will be the appropriate
form of an increasingly residualised public sector. Attention
is beginning to be given to these issues but research and
debate still have a very long way to go.

Anderson, J., Duncan, S. and Hudson, R. (1983) Redundant
    Spaces in Cities and Regions?, Academic Press, London
Association of Metropolitan Authorities (1982a, 1983) Housing
    Capital Expenditure Survey, unpublished
Association of Metropolitan Authorities (1982b) The Rate
    Support Grant Settlement 1982-83: A Guide for Local
    Authorities, AMA, London
Audit Commission (1986) Managing the Crisis in Council
    Housing, HMSO, London
Balbo, L. (1982) 'The Servicing Work of Women and the
    Capitalist State' in M. Zeitlin (ed.) Political Power
    and Social Theory, JAI Press, London
Ball, M. (1982) 'Housing Provision and the Economic Crisis',
    Capital and Class, 17, 66-77
Ball, M. (1983) Housing Policy and Economic Power, Methuen,
    London
Bank of England (1982) 'Mortgage Lending and the Housing
    Market', Bank of England Quarterly Bulletin, 22, 390-8.
Barclay, P. (1982) Social Workers: Their Role and Tasks,
    Bedford Square Press, London
Blunkett, D. and Green, G. (1983) Building from the Bottom:
    The Sheffield Experience, Fabian Society, London
Brion, M. and Tinker, A. (1980) Women in Housing: Access and
    Influence, Housing Centre Trust, London
Building Societies Association (1983) Housing Tenure, BSA,
    London
Central Housing Advisory Committee (1938) Management of
    Municipal Estates, HMSO, London
Clapham, D. and Maclennan, D. (1983) 'Residualisation of
    Public Housing: A Non-Issue', Housing Review, 32, 9-10
Clapham, D., Kintrea, K., Millar, M. and Munro, M. (1985)
    Co-operative Housing in Norway and Sweden, Centre for
    Housing Research, University of Glasgow
Clapham, D. and Kintrea, K. (1986) 'Rationing, Choice and
    Constraint: The Allocation of Public Housing in
    Glasgow', Journal of Social Policy, 15, 51-67
Cockburn, C. (1977) The Local State: Management of Cities
    and People, Pluto, London
Coleman, A. (1985) Utopia on Trial: Vision and Reality in
    Planned Housing, Hilary Shipman, London
Cowan, R. (1985) 'Ill Wind in the Willows', Roof, 10, 11-14
Damer, S. and Madigan, R. (1974) 'The Housing Investigator',
    New Society, 29, 226-7
Daunton, M. (ed.) (1984) Councillors and Tenants: Local
    Authority Housing in English Cities, 1919-1939,
    Leicester University Press, Leicester
Department of the Environment (1977) Housing Policy:
    Technical Volume, HMSO, London

Department of the Environment (1982) English House Condition
    Survey, 1981: Part I, HMSO, London
Department of the Environment (1985) Housing and Construction
    Statistics, 1974-1984, HMSO, London
Donnison, D. (1967) The Government of Housing, Penguin,
    Harmondsworth
Duclaud-Williams, R. (1978) The Politics of Housing in
    Britain and France, Heinemann, London
Dunleavy, P. (1980) Urban Political Analysis, Macmillan,
    London
Dunnell, K. (1979) Family Formation 1976, HMSO, London
English, J. (1982a) 'Must Council Housing Become Welfare
    Housing?', Housing Review, 31, 154-6, 212-13
English, J. (ed.) (1982b) The Future of Council Housing, Croom
    Helm, London
English, J. (forthcoming) 'Access to Public Sector Housing'
    in M. Pacione (ed.), Progress in Human Geography,
    Croom Helm, London
Ermisch, J. (1984) Housing Finance: Who Gains?, Policy
    Studies Institute, London
Fielding, N. (1984) 'Who is Subsidising Whom?', Roof, 9, 11-14
Figeat, D. (1983) 'Housing Improvement Policy in France' in
    Urban Capital Finance, Organisation for Economic
    Co-operation and Development, Paris
Forrest, R., Lansley, S. and Murie, A. (1984) A Foot on the
    Ladder?: An Evaluation of Low Cost Home Ownership
    Initiatives, School for Advanced Urban Studies,
    University of Bristol
Forrest, R. and Murie, A. (1983) 'Residualisation and Council
    Housing: Aspects of Changing Social Relations of
    Housing and Tenure', Journal of Social Policy, 12,
    453-68
Forrest, R. and Murie, A. (1984a) Monitoring the Right to Buy
    1980-82, School for Advanced Urban Studies, University
    of Bristol
Forrest, R. and Murie, A. (1984b) Right to Buy? Issues of
    Need, Equity and Polarisation in the Sale of Council
    Houses, School for Advanced Urban Studies, University
    of Bristol
Forrest, R. and Murie, A. (forthcoming), Selling the Welfare
    State, Croom Helm, London
Great Britain (1977) Housing Policy: A Consultative
    Document, Cmnd. 6851, HMSO, London
Great Britain (1985) The Government's Expenditure Plans
    1985-86 to 1987-88, Cmnd. 9428, HMSO, London
Grey, A., Hepworth, N. and Odling-Smee, J. (1978) Housing
    Rents, Costs and Subsidies, Chartered Institute of
    Public Finance and Accountancy, London
Grosskurth, A. (1982) Local Authority-Private Sector
    Partnership in Inner City Development, unpublished
    M.Phil thesis, University College London
Hadley, R. and Hatch, S. (1981) Social Welfare and the
    Failure of the State, Allen and Unwin, London

Bibliography

Hague, C. (1985) 'Housing Privatisation in Practice', Housing and Planning Review, 40, 16-18

Hambleton, R. (1978) Policy Planning and Local Government, Hutchinson, London

Hamnett, C. (1983a) 'Split City', Roof, 8, 13-14

Hamnett, C. (1983b) 'The New Geography of Housing', New Society, 66, 396-8

Hamnett, C. (1984) 'Housing the Two Nations: Socio-Tenurial Polarisation in England and Wales, 1961-1981', Urban Studies, 43, 389-405

Hamnett, C. and Randolph, W. (1983a) 'The Changing Tenure Structure of the Greater London Housing Market, 1961-81', The London Journal, 9, 153-164

Hamnett, C. and Randolph, W. (1983b) 'The Flat Breakers', London Housing, 25, 6-7

Hamnett, C. and Randolph, W. (1984) 'The Role of Landlord Disinvestment in Housing Market Transformation: An Analysis of Flat Break-up in Central London', Transactions of the Institute of British Geographers, New Series, 9, 259-279

Hamnett, C. and Randolph, W. (1986) 'The Role of Housing and Labour Markets in the Production of Geographical Variations in Social Stratification', in K. Hoggart and E. Kofman (eds.), Politics, Geography and Social Stratification, Croom Helm, London

Harloe, M. (1978a), 'Housing and the State: Recent British Developments', International Social Science Journal, XXX, 591-603

Harloe, M. (1978b) 'The Green Paper on Housing Policy' in M. Brown and S. Baldwin (eds.), The Yearbook of Social Policy in Britain, Routledge and Kegan Paul, London

Harloe, M. (1981) 'The Recommodification of Housing' in M. Harloe and E. Lebas (eds.), City, Class and Capital, Edward Arnold, London

Harloe, M. (1982) 'Towards the Decommodification of Housing? A Comment on Council House Sales', Critical Social Policy, 2, 39-42

Harloe, M. (1984) Private Rented Housing in the United States and Europe, Croom Helm, London

Harloe, M. and Martens, M. (1984) 'Comparative Housing Research', Journal of Social Policy, 13, 255-77

Harloe, M. and Martens, M. (1985) 'The Restructuring of Housing Provision in Britain and the Netherlands', Environment and Planning A, 17, 1063-87

Heald, D. (1983) Public Expenditure, Martin Robertson, Oxford

Henderson, J. and Karn, V. (1986) Race, Class and State Housing, Gower, Aldershot

Henney, A. (1985) Trust the Tenant: Devolving Municipal Housing, Centre for Policy Studies, London

Hill, O. (1875) Houses of the London Poor, Macmillan, London

Holmans, A. (1981) 'Housing Careers of Recently Married Couples', Population Trends, 24, 10-14

Bibliography

House of Commons (1980) Environment Committee: First Report, Session 1979-80, HC 714, HMSO, London

Housing Research Group, City University (1981) Could Local Authorities Be Better Landlords?, City University, London

Howenstine, E. (1975) 'The Changing Roles of Housing Production Subsidies and Consumer Housing Subsidies in European National Housing Policy', Land Economics, 51, 86-94

Howenstine, E. (1983) Attacking Housing Costs: Foreign Policies and Strategies, Centre for Urban Policy Research, New Brunswick

Ineichen, J. (1980) The Housing Decisions of Young People, unpublished mimeo

Inquiry into British Housing, (1985) The Evidence, National Federation of Housing Associations, London

Institute of Housing (1984) Housing Capital Expenditure, IOH, London

Jenkin, P. (1985) Speech for Institute of Housing, Department of the Environment, mimeo

Johnson, C. (1984) 'Borrowing Without Tears', Lloyds Bank Economic Bulletin, 62

Jowell, R. and Airey, C. (1984) British Social Attitudes: the 1984 Report, Gower, Aldershot

Kemeny, J. (1981) The Myth of Home Ownership, Routledge and Kegan Paul, London

Kemeny, J. and Thomas, A. (1984) 'Capital Leakage from Owner-Occupied Housing', Policy and Politics, 12, 13-30

Madge, J. and Brown, C. (1981) First Homes, Policy Studies Institute, London

Malpass, P. (1984) 'Octavia Hill', in P. Barker (ed.) Founders of the Welfare State, Heinemann, London

Malpass, P. (1983) 'Residualisation and the Restructuring of Housing Tenure', Housing Review, 32, 44-5

Martens, M. (1985) 'Owner Occupied Housing in Europe: Post War Developments and Current Dilemmas', Environment and Planning A, 17, 605-24.

Massey, D. (1983) 'The Shape of Things to Come', Marxism Today, XXVII, 18-27

McCulloch, D. (1981) 'Housing Finance: A One-Sided Approach?', Housing Review, 30, 184-5

McQueen, W. (1983) Movement into and within the Owner Occupied Sector of the Housing Market, Central Research Unit, Scottish Office, Edinburgh

Merrett, S. (1982) Owner Occupation in Britain, Routledge and Kegan Paul, London

Moberly Bell, E. (1942) Octavia Hill, Constable, London

Mosely, R. (1984) 'Liberating the Public Sector' in Labour Housing Group, Right to a Home, Spokesman, Nottingham

Murie, A. (1982) 'A New Era for Council Housing?' in J. English (ed.) The Future of Council Housing, Croom Helm, London

Murie, A. (1983) Housing Inequality and Deprivation,
    Heinemann, London
Murie, A. and Forrest, R. (1980) 'Wealth, Inheritance and
    Social Policy', Policy and Politics, 8, 1-19
Murie, A., Niner, P. and Watson, C. (1976) Housing Policy and
    the Housing System, Allen and Unwin, London
Nabarro, R. (1980) 'The Impact on Workers from the Inner City
    of Liverpool's Economic Decline' in A. Evans and D.
    Eversley (eds.), The Inner City, Heinemann, London
National Consumer Council (1979) Soonest Mended, NCC, London
Offe, C. (1984) Contradictions of the Welfare State,
    Hutchinson, London
Office of Population Censuses and Surveys (1982) Housing and
    Households, HMSO, London
Office of Population Censuses and Surveys (1984) Census 1981:
    Household and Family Composition Tables: England and
    Wales, HMSO, London
Office of Population Censuses and Surveys (1984) Social
    Trends 1983, HMSO, London
Payne, J. and Payne, G. (1977) 'Housing Pathways and
    Stratification: A Study of Life Chances in the
    Housing Market', Journal of Social Policy, 6, 129-56
Pearsall, J. (1984) 'France', in M. Wynn (ed.), Housing in
    Europe, Croom Helm, London
Pfeiffer, U. and Stahl, K. (1975) 'Housing Finance Policies
    in Germany' in M. Whitbread (ed.) Housing Finance
    Policies: An International Review, Centre for
    Environmental Studies, London
Power, A. (1984) Local Housing Management: A Priority
    Estates Project Survey, Department of the Environment,
    London
Priemus, H. (1981) 'Rent and Subsidy Policy in the
    Netherlands during the Seventies', Urban Law and
    Policy, 4, 299-355
Rigby, R. (1982) The Residents as Resource: A Public Housing
    Management Demonstration in Jersey City, Department of
    Community Affairs, Trenton
Robinson, R. and O'Sullivan, T. (1983) 'Housing Tenure
    Polarisation: Some Empirical Evidence', Housing
    Review, 32, 116-17
Runnymede Trust (1975) Race and Council Housing in London,
    Runnymede Trust, London
Saunders, P. (1984) 'Beyond Housing Classes: The
    Sociological Significance of Private Property Rights
    and Means of Consumption', International Journal of
    Urban and Social Research, 8, 202-27
Scottish Consumer Council (1983) Terms of Tenancy: An
    Analysis of New Leases Issued to Public Sector Tenants
    in Scotland, SCC, Glasgow
Scottish Development Department (1985) Scottish Housing
    Statistics 1984, HMSO, Edinburgh

Bibliography

Seabrook, J. (1984) The Idea of Neighbourhood, Pluto, London
Seebohm (1968) Report of the Committee on Local Authority and Allied Personal Social Services, Cmnd. 3703, HMSO, London
Sullivan, O. and Murphy, M. (1984) 'Housing Pathways and Stratification: Some Evidence from a British National Survey', Journal of Social Policy, 13, 147-165
Szelenyi, I. (1981) 'Alternatives to Capitalist Development: An Agenda for Urban Research', International Journal of Urban and Regional Research, 5, 1-14
Titmuss, R. (1958) Essays on the Welfare State, Allen and Unwin, London
Tucker, J. (1966) Honourable Estates, Gollancz, London
Turner, J. (1972) Housing by People: Towards Autonomy in Building Environments, Marion Boyars, London
United Nations Economic Commission for Europe (1949) The European Housing Problem: A Preliminary Review, UN, Geneva
United Nations Economic Commission for Europe (1954) European Housing Progress and Policies in 1953, UN, Geneva
United Nations Economic Commission for Europe (1958) The Financing of Housing in Europe, UN, Geneva
United Nations Economic Commission for Europe (1973) Financing of Housing, UN, Geneva
United Nations Economic Commission for Europe (1976) Human Settlements in Europe: Post-War Trends and Policies, UN, New York
United Nations Economic Commission for Europe (1980) Major Trends in Housing Policy in ECE Countries, UN, New York
Ward, C. (1974) Tenants Take Over, Architectural Press, London
Warnes, A. and Law, C. (1984) 'The Elderly Population of Great Britain: Locational Trends and Policy Implications', Transactions of the Institute of British Geographers, New Series, 9, 37-59
Watson, C. (1977) 'Housing Policy and the Sale of Council Houses' in J. English and C. Jones (eds.), The Sale of Council Houses, Department of Social and Economic Research, University of Glasgow
Webster, D. (1981) 'A "Social Market" Answer on Housing', New Society, 58, 269-72
White, M. (1983) Long-Term Unemployment and Labour Markets, Policy Studies Institute, London
Whitehead, C. (1983) 'Privatisation and Housing' in J. Le Grand and R. Robinson (eds.) Privatisation and the Welfare State, Allen and Unwin, London
Whitfield, D. (1983) Making It Public, Pluto, London
Wynn, M. (ed.) (1984) Housing in Europe, Croom Helm, London
Young, K. and Kramer, J. (1978) Strategy and Conflict in Metropolitan Housing, Heinemann, London

Index

Index

Industrialised building: <u>see</u> systems-building
Institute of Housing 5, 56
Institute of Housing Administration 109
Islington 151, 152, 159
Italy 142

Jenkin, P. 2, 5, 64

Labour government (1974-79) 51, 90
Labour Housing Group 145
Labour party 4, 128, 146, 151
Lambeth 42-4, 46, 50
Langbaurgh 10, 147
Liverpool 14, 15, 25-9, 147, 155
Local Contribution Differential (LCD) 57
London 15, 23-5, 29, 38, 153
London Borough Association 63

Marginalisation 27, 34, 69, 72, 73, 80, 82, 84, 85, 130
Municipalisation 55

National Health Service 112
National Mobility Scheme 7, 8
National Movers Survey (1973) 20
Netherlands 126, 127, 128, 129, 132, 133, 134, 136, 139, 142
New Commonwealth 42, 44, 48
New Forest 77
New Towns 90, 92, 94, 96, 100, 102, 103
Norway 164

Owner occupation 12, 14, 17, 29, 61, 97, 129, 132, 140, 141, 144; desire for 2, 68, 69, 81, 82; <u>see also</u> sale of council houses

Pakistan 42, 44, 48

Participation of tenants: 118, 119, 139, 143, 145, 160, 163, <u>see also</u> housing management
Peripheral estates 26, 84, 131
Polarisation 20, 25, 29, 38, 50, 149, 161, 164; background to 14, 15; context of 34; definition of 3; impact of 12, 13; in Inner London 43; measurement of 16, 17, 18, 36, 37; socio-economic structure and 38, 39, 45-7; spatial dimension of 22, 23, 74
Priority Estates Project (PEP) 118, 119, 120, 121, 122, 152, 157, 159
Private rented sector 1, 2, 4, 35, 84
Privatisation 68-70, 81, 85 146, 147, 149, 150, 154, 156, 158, 159
Public sector housing 2, 12, 33, 87, 140-2; access to 5, 6, 131; and privatisation 23, 26, 27; factors in decline of European 130-4; organisation of 127, 132, 138; repair and maintenance of 110, 111, 115, 118, 122, 130-4, 150, 152, 153, 157; sale of:<u>see</u> sale of council houses

Rate-capping 56, 60
Rate Fund Contributions (RFC) 51, 53, 56, 58, 59, 60-4, 66
Rate Support Grant (RSG) 53, 56, 58, 59, 60, 61, 62, 63
Rent 51, 53, 56, 60, 122 132, 142, 146, 154;